"Jesus was not a white 1
He called for a revolution, ... -
establishment. *Manifesto* carries on the revolution started
by Jesus. Olu Robbin-Coker, an African living in Europe,
captures the heart of the revolution. He understands
the non-Western, non-white heart of our faith. He calls
us to repudiate religion and follow Jesus. Run, don't
walk, to the nearest bookstore and buy this book!"

—Floyd McClung
International Director of All Nations

"I have known Olu since his university years at St.
Andrews, and he has demonstrated a deep commitment
to Christian discipleship throughout that time. Olu is a
man of integrity, and he lives out what he teaches. His
passion has inspired many young people to live completely for God. I warmly commend his book to you."

—Wade Robertson
South African missionary for 30 years

"*Manifesto* is a unique book with valuable insights for
anyone who wants to know Jesus more and join in
the wonderful and sometimes arduous journey of
church and its role in bringing the hope and grace
of the Gospel to every area of culture and society.
Olu's journey of faith is compelling and his story
is refreshing. I'm glad to call him my friend."

—Tre Sheppard
Lead singer, Onehundredhours

"What I really appreciate about Olu's *Manifesto* is that it reads like an unfolding conversation rather than a strict religious creed. Here is one believer unpacking his spiritual pilgrimage for the rest of us, and inviting us into the journey with him. I count it a real honour to have travelled part of this journey with Olu and an even greater honour to call him my friend."

—Trent Sheppard
Status teaching pastor and YWAM speaker

"Olu teaches the way Jesus advocates in John 7:17 when Jesus said that the only way to learn true doctrine was to be willing to do his Father's will. Olu's fascinating journey of faith and discipleship, which he tells in this book, opens up and illuminates the excitement of a life with Jesus. As he obeys, he understands, and makes us hungry to follow Christ also. A great inspirational read."

—Roger Forster
Cofounder, Ichthus Christian Fellowship

OLU ROBBIN-COKER

MANIFESTO

REVOLUTIONARY CHRISTIANITY FOR A POSTMODERN WORLD

P.O. BOX 55787 / SEATTLE, WA 98155

YWAM Publishing is the publishing ministry of Youth With A Mission. Youth With A Mission (YWAM) is an international missionary organization of Christians from many denominations dedicated to presenting Jesus Christ to this generation. To this end, YWAM has focused its efforts in three main areas: (1) training and equipping believers for their part in fulfilling the Great Commission (Matthew 28:19), (2) personal evangelism, and (3) mercy ministry (medical and relief work).

For a free catalog of books and materials, call (425) 771-1153 or (800) 922-2143. Visit us online at www.ywampublishing.com.

Manifesto: Revolutionary Christianity for a Postmodern World
Copyright © 2008 by Olu Robbin-Coker
Published by YWAM Publishing
P.O. Box 55787, Seattle, WA 98155

Unless otherwise noted, Scripture quotations in this book are taken from the World English Bible. For information, visit http://ebible.org.

Library of Congress Cataloging-in-Publication Data

Robbin-Coker, Olu.
    Manifesto : revolutionary Christianity for a postmodern world / Olu Robbin-Coker.
        p. cm.
    ISBN 978-1-57658-471-2
    1. Spirituality. 2. Spiritual life. 3. Christian life. 4. Postmodernism—Religious aspects—Christianity. I. Title.
    BV4501.3.R625 2008
    270.8'3—dc22   2008035060

14 13 12 11 10 09 08   10 9 8 7 6 5 4 3 2 1

ISBN 978-1-57658-471-2

Printed in the United States of America

To Ester, Rebekah, Sophia, and Daniel
To all those who have set their hearts on pilgrimage
To the orphans of Sierra Leone
To all the less fortunate children of God

Contents

Acknowledgments

Massive thanks go to everyone who has helped make this book a reality. I particularly want to thank Frank Kremer, Kirsten Walker, Charis Robertson, Fiona Dixon, and Webster Simpson for their hard work. I owe you big time. Thanks to my brother Christian for encouragement that kept me going when I wanted to give up. Thanks to Mummy and Daddy, Sanya, Niyi, and Morenike for always believing in me.

Thanks to the people at YWAM Publishing who helped make this dream a reality: Tom Bragg, Ryan Davis, and others.

I especially need to thank Ester and the girls for putting up with my absences, mood swings, and other endearing qualities.

Thanks to Libby and kids, Ted and family.

Thanks to YWAM, Community Church Dundee, and The Revolution.

Acknowledgements

Introduction

An Englishman in New York? Not really. But certainly an African in Scotland. This year will be the year that I have spent an equal amount of time in the UK and my home country of Sierra Leone—sixteen years in each. It may be no coincidence that my first foray into publishing comes at this time: I have the unusual privilege of looking at the world through two hugely different worldviews. I hope to end up with some kind of 3-D image.

The purpose of this book is to share the journey of discovery that God has taken me on the past few years. A key word to describe this journey is *convergence*. Although I was christened and confirmed in the Anglican Church, I was converted in a Pentecostal church and baptized in a charismatic church. Along the way I have learned many positive things from each of these traditions, and more than that, the traditions have come together in my life to produce what I can only describe as a "convergent Christian."

My beliefs and my practices have changed so much from when I first embarked on this journey that it sometimes seems as if my faith is completely different from what it first was. The difference between my present faith and my initial faith is that my initial faith was handed down to me without my questioning any of it, whereas my present faith is one that I have painstakingly uncovered through my personal journey with the help of many other Christians. I still have a lot of the hand-me-down faith, but it no longer makes up the majority of my faith.

On this journey I have had a question answered that I was not expecting. I only recently started asking the question and have realized that God has been slowly answering the question all along. The question is very simple: how can I be a radical Christian in a postmodern world? In this book I want to share with you what I have learned about this on my journey. Along the way I have drawn some conclusions, and more conclusions are yet to be drawn. I would like to share both with you: the conclusions and the remaining questions.

So how did my journey begin? It started in earnest with an argument. It was a wonderful evening of conversation with a friend which sadly ended in a row about theology. I wish I could say this was unusual for me, but at that time I had heated debates at least every other week, if not every week. My friend challenged my theology in such a major way that I responded not just in anger but with real arrogance. I thought that what he was proposing was so off the wall that it was stupid even to believe it. The source of contention was about my view of the nature and character of God. I left my friend that day with a resolve to prove him wrong, and I embarked on my first major study of the Bible.

Over a period of months, maybe even a year, of Bible study and book reading, I came to the conclusion that my friend was right. This learning process made me realize that I had little basis for many of my beliefs, except to say, "This is what I was taught." An answer like that did not really give a reason for the hope that I possessed (1 Pet. 3:15).

Since that season of my life, I have been on a continuous journey to know God better and to know what I believe personally rather than what I have been told to believe. My Christian journey has been characterized by some major paradigm shifts, resulting in an approach to the Christian walk that is not very mainstream in the context of where I live today. This has been a necessary step for me on my journey to being a radical Christian in a postmodern world.

To be radical Christians in a postmodern world, we must undergo a process of rebirth. We need Jesus to prune all the extra bits that he never gave us to carry. We need to embrace the simplicity of following his leading. This simplicity will enable us to function effectively as Christians in our given contexts. But if we find that we cannot live out our faith effectively in any context, we must question what kind of faith we have adopted.

As indicated above, the purpose of this book is not so much to give answers to questions as it is to generate questions. Every individual is a unique creation of God and has a unique personality and a unique relationship with God. It is therefore important that all individuals embark on a journey of discovery where they can look to God, themselves, and the body of Christ to figure out what they believe and where God is taking them.

On my journey, not only my doctrine has changed but also my practice of faith. Any doctrine that does not affect the way we live falls short of Christ's intention. As James said, we are not only to be hearers of the word but also doers, otherwise we become deceived (James 1:22).

As I have journeyed with God, I have developed some foundational thoughts that shape my Christian walk. In fact, I have ended up with something of a manifesto divided into four sections—up, down, in, and out. Each section depicts a direction we must look as we follow Christ:

We need to look **UP** to God. This section focuses on how we see God and on the resulting relationship we can have with him when we have a right view of who he is.

We need to look **DOWN** into ourselves. This section focuses on Christians as individuals—our walk with God and the path of spiritual growth.

We need to look **IN** to the church. This section examines the corporate Christian life—what it means to be church and what our gatherings and ministries could look like.

We need to look **OUT** to the world. This section discusses how each of us can impact the world around us and advance the kingdom of God on the earth.

Join me as I share my manifesto.

UP

Section A

Look UP to God

1. Discovering Love

The most life-changing step on my journey toward God has been discovering the loving nature and character of all three persons of the Godhead. I remember distinctly the start of one of the most marvelous seasons of my Christian life. I was a student at university, and one of my friends from church organized three Sundays of showing videotapes by Mike Bickle speaking on the subject of his well-known book *Passion for Jesus*. I expected Bickle to teach "three easy steps" to becoming more passionate about God and becoming an "on-fire Christian." But instead he taught that *Jesus* was on fire with passion for his bride—and that included me.

A major insight like this tends to send me to my Bible to search out what truth there is in the message. It is not enough for me just to like the sound of a teaching; I have to know whether it is true and whether it can be confirmed in the Bible. This particular teaching sounded almost too good to be true.

Too often I find that people think that if they believe something and want it bad enough, it will become true. That may sound ridiculous, but we all do it to some degree. Here's an example: No matter how much someone might want to believe it, I am not a white female. If because of poor eyesight or a psychological problem someone thinks that I am a white female, that does not change the reality that I am a black male. Truth cannot be created by our desires. God, then, will not change to accommodate our incorrect beliefs; rather, we must change our thinking to line up with the reality of who he is.

Back to the story. As a result of the videos and my personal times of prayer, Bible study, and other reading, I discovered a Jesus that I had never known. He was warm and tender. He was the lover of my soul. I realized that I had a deep longing in my soul to be loved and accepted, and to find out that I was loved and accepted by the most significant Threesome in the universe was mind altering. In the weeks following, I experienced what I can only describe as a "baptism of love." I walked around like a love-struck teenager for months. This baptism is something I have never recovered from and never want to recover from.

Spreading the Word

Do you remember what it was like as a teenager when you thought you were in love? You had real excitement about the object of your affection, and you talked about that person all the time. You wanted to be around the person constantly. You quite gladly told everyone how wonderful your loved one was. You were not ashamed of the one you loved; on the contrary, you wanted to shout his or her name from the rooftops. Even if you were usually self-conscious, you gladly walked down the street holding hands with your loved one. You wanted the entire world to see that "my beloved is mine, and I am his" (Song of Sol. 2:16).

My life had begun to change as the truth of God's love became a reality to me. I became so confident about God's love and acceptance that I wanted others to know. I preached about God's love and grace to anyone who would listen. It really did not matter whether you were a Christian; you were going to hear that God loved you.

One of the reasons that many people struggle to talk about their faith is that they have not experienced the good news they are trying to communicate. How can we ever truly speak of the goodness of God's unconditional love for humankind if we have not experienced it ourselves? I believe that God wants us to experience his love in such a real way that telling people about a God of love becomes a natural thing for us to do. When you have met Jesus, you have to tell someone about it. When you have experienced forgiveness of sins, you have to tell others. When you have experienced God's grace, you have to spread the word.

I had experienced something that I felt everyone needed to experience. God's love for me has continued to be the driving force behind my faith. The fact that the almighty God, Creator of the universe, loves me so much that he was willing to die for me is enough to keep me going not only in this life but in the life to come.

The Nature of God

From my study of the Word and my experiences, I concluded that love is central not only to the Christian life but also to the character of God. I think the Bible agrees with me on this point (or is it the other way around?).

In the New Testament, the apostle John provides three very direct statements about God that give us a glimpse of what God is like. The first statement occurs in the context of worship. In John 4, Jesus tells the Samaritan woman that "God is spirit, and those who worship him must worship in spirit and truth" (verse 24). The statement "God is spirit" speaks of the very nature and substance of God. He is not human, consisting of flesh and blood, but is a spiritual being composed entirely of spirit. The technical language I have learned to describe us and God is: we are made of human stuff and God is made of God stuff. This God stuff could be called Eternal Uncreated Spirit.

We find the next statement in 1 John 1: "God is light and in him is no darkness at all" (verse 5). This statement gives us an insight into the mind of God, so to speak. God's mind is a perfect mind in which all things are clear and no errors of judgment are made. He is perfect in all his ways and knows all things there are to be known. One of the few limitations we would dare put on God's knowledge of all things is that God has no intimate knowledge of sin. We could therefore say: he knows all things that will not cause any darkness to enter his light. This knowledge will serve no useful purpose so he chooses not to know it. He does, however, know what it is like to be tempted by sin through the incarnation of Jesus.

The final statement is "God is love," found in 1 John 4 (verses 8 and 16). Of all the statements about God, this one took me the longest to get to grips with. It is one thing to say that God is a loving God, but it is much stronger to say that God is love itself. I believe that this statement speaks of the character of God—what he is like as a person and how he relates to his creation. I will discuss this in more detail shortly.

As I meditated on these and other scriptures, such as Exodus 34, I realized that God is not who I thought he was. Before, it sometimes felt as if God was the angry ogre in the sky, controlling everything and everyone and occasionally throwing a cosmic tantrum that resulted in disasters like the Flood. But I came to see him as an extremely caring and generous God who is motivated primarily by love, and even his seemingly cruel actions are part of a cosmic plan motivated by a love for the entirety of his creation.

God Is Love

The statement "God is love" is unique. There are scriptures that talk about God being loving (Exod. 34:6; John 3:16), but this scripture says that he *is* love and that whoever lives in love lives in God and God in him (1 John 4:16). Such strong statements about God must not be ignored, especially when viewed alongside other scriptures. For example, in Ephesians 3:16–19 Paul says that when we fully experience the love of God, we will attain to the fullness of God. *Fullness* is no small thing, and the Bible says that the fullness of God is found in *love*.

The Scriptures emphasize no other character attributes of God at such a level. They might say that God is caring (1 Pet 5:7) but not that God is care, or even that God is just (Isa. 45:21) but not that God is justice. They might say that God is gracious (2 Chron. 30:9) but not that God is grace. Get my point?

We cannot afford to ignore the Scriptures as we try to understand God's character. Because God is love, we can feel safe and at home with him, not constantly trembling in fear. As the writer of Hebrews says, we can boldly approach the throne (Heb. 4:16). Why? Because of what Christ has done for us. And why did Christ do this? Because of love.

John says that God is love and that if we claim we know God but do not display love, we cannot be telling the truth.

21

Here's the way I see it: if God is love and we are truly born of God, then we will naturally display love. Love will be something that is in our nature. As people often say, like produces like; you cannot get pineapples from a mango tree. This, I believe, is why Jesus said, "By this everyone will know that you are my disciples, if you have love for one another" (John 13:35).

Defining Love

I am sometimes accused of softening God and making him out to be some wet and soppy God, but I do not believe this is the case. The reason people get nervous about my emphasis on God's love is that they have misunderstood biblical love. Instead of taking their definition of love from the Bible, many people have consciously or subconsciously taken on the world's values and views of love.

By exploring some attributes of love, we can better understand it. I could spend a whole book talking about this, but I will highlight just a few points about love that influence the way we see God.

Looking at 1 Corinthians 13, we see that love is patient. God's patience and kindness have continually amazed me, because if anyone is justified in being impatient with humans, it is the perfect God who makes no mistakes. Because of his patience, God waits for a rebellious world to come to repentance instead of judging the world right now. Jesus also reflected God's patience with humanity in the gentle way that he related to sinners. The people he tended to be hard on were the hypocritical religious leaders of the time. In my life, I have seen how God has patiently waited for me to come around to his way of thinking.

God is also selfless. His purposes in loving us are not for personal gain. What could God, who has everything, gain from us? God's agenda for an earth filled with his glory is not because he needs his ego massaged. Love does not boast and is not prideful. God desires what is best for us, and what is best for us is a kingdom in which God rules benevolently.

The ultimate display of God's sacrificial love is the Cross. The Cross is the most selfless act this world has ever known. Many people talk about love as a feeling they have or a need they require to be fulfilled. But God is in a relationship with us not because of what he can get from us but because of what he can give to us.

Many people live in fear of God's wrath toward sin. Some may view God as an ill-tempered dad who is just waiting for an excuse to punish his family. Such fear of God does not foster the kind of relationship God wants to have with his children.

I am moved deeply by the fact that God is not easily angered. If God *were* easily annoyed by me and my many mistakes, I would be a goner. But the Bible promises that we can boldly approach the throne of God because of what Christ has done for us. We do not have a father who is looking for a reason to punish us. On the contrary, our Father is looking for a reason to forgive us, and that reason is Christ and his work on the Cross. God is quick to forgive those who seek his forgiveness. John writes, "If we confess our sins, he is faithful and righteous to forgive us the sins, and to cleanse us from all unrighteousness" (1 John 1:9). And as God forgives, he chooses not to remember. He keeps no record of wrongs.

I once heard this story: A Christian man was struggling with a particular sin in his life. One day he sought God with all his heart for forgiveness. The man truly felt God's forgiveness and resolved not to commit this particular sin again. A few days went by and he found himself stumbling again. He got on his knees before God and said, "Lord, please forgive me. I have done it again." Then he heard the still small voice of the Lord ask, "Done what again?"

When God forgives our sins, he means it and chooses not to count them against us in the future. Every day is a new day with God.

People often view love in a romantic, unreal, Hollywood-type way, where love is the passion that two people have for each other or the act of letting the object of one's love do what he or she wants. Such views fall short of the biblical concept of love. First Corinthians 13 gives a wonderful description of love and therefore, by inference, describes God's character:

> Love is patient and is kind; love doesn't envy. Love doesn't brag, is not proud, doesn't behave itself inappropriately, doesn't seek its own way, is not provoked, takes no account of evil; doesn't rejoice in unrighteousness, but rejoices with the truth; bears all things, believes all things, hopes all things, endures all things. Love never fails. (1 Cor. 13:4–8)

Some people might conclude that my emphasis on God as love does not make room for God's wrath, anger, or even justice. I have heard statements such as, "We have to balance God's love with his anger." I think life would be a lot different if God's wrath and love were "equal" as these people suggest. The reason someone would say this is that they have misunderstood the source and purpose of God's anger. The Bible indicates that God becomes angry because of evil that is going on. The statement "Love [and therefore God] does not delight in evil but rejoices with the truth" (1 Cor. 13:6 NIV) confirms this fact. The interesting thing, then, is that God's wrath is because of his love and not in spite of it. Although this is hard to get our heads around, it is worthy of our meditation. God is angry because he is love. He is angry at the destructive nature of sin. It is difficult for us as flawed humans to understand the righteous anger of God contained within his love.

The Discipline of Love

Because of his love and his hatred of evil, God finds it necessary to discipline his children. Again, if your view of love is based on worldly values, then you will find the idea of discipline and punishment from God a difficult one. But if you understand love from a biblical point of view, you do not have the same difficulty.

Sometimes I hear people say, "If God loves me, why am I going through such difficult times?" This kind of statement reveals a person's misunderstanding of God's love and also of Christianity as a whole.

"For whom the Lord loves, he chastens, and scourges every son whom he receives." It is for discipline that you endure. God deals with you as with children, for what son is there whom his father doesn't discipline? But if you are without discipline, of which all have been made partakers, then are you illegitimate, and not children. Furthermore, we had the fathers of our flesh to chasten us, and we paid them respect. Shall we not much rather be in subjection to the Father of spirits, and live? For they indeed, for a few days, punished us as seemed good to them; but he for our profit, that we may be partakers of his holiness. All chastening seems for the present to be not joyous but grievous; yet afterward it yields the peaceful fruit of righteousness to those who have been exercised thereby. (Heb. 12:6–11)

In the history of God's relationship with Israel, God allowed or caused difficulty in order that his children might learn. Even Jesus "learned obedience by the things which he suffered" (Heb. 5:8). None of us—whether a nation or an individual— can escape the discipline of God if we are truly his children. For God *not* to discipline us would mean he does not love us. We often forget that God's goal for us is not comfort but growth into maturity.

Count it all joy, my brothers, when you fall into various temptations, knowing that the testing of your faith produces endurance. Let endurance have its perfect work, that you may be perfect and complete, lacking in nothing. (James 1:2–4)

Ezekiel's Love Story

God's love is not all the scary stuff of discipline; it also contains within it some very delicate touches. I would even dare to say that some romantic elements come across. One of my favorite scriptures indicating the delicate nature of God's love for Israel is in Ezekiel 16.

Thus says the Lord Yahweh to Jerusalem: Your birth and your birth is of the land of the Canaanite; the Amorite was your father, and your mother was a Hittite. As for your birth, in the day you were born your navel was not cut, neither were you washed in water to cleanse you; you weren't salted at all, nor swaddled at all. No eye pitied you, to do any of these things to you, to have compassion on you; but you were cast out in the open field, for that your person was abhorred, in the day that you were born. When I passed by you, and saw you wallowing in your blood, I said to you, Though you are in your blood, live; yes, I said to you, Though you are in your blood, live. I caused you to multiply as that which grows in the field, and you increased and grew great, and you attained to excellent ornament; your breasts were fashioned, and your hair was grown; yet you were naked and bare. Now when I passed by you, and looked at you, behold, your time was the time of love; and I spread my skirt over you, and covered your nakedness: yes, I swore to you, and entered into a covenant with you, says the Lord Yahweh, and you became mine. Then washed I you with water; yes, I thoroughly washed away your blood from you, and I anointed you with oil. I clothed you also with embroidered work, and shod you with sealskin, and I dressed you about with fine linen, and covered you with silk. I decked you with ornaments, and I put bracelets on your hands, and a chain on your neck. I put a ring on your nose, and earrings in your ears, and a beautiful crown on your head. Thus you were decked with gold and silver; and your clothing was of fine linen, and silk, and embroidered work; you ate fine flour, and honey, and oil; and you were exceeding beautiful, and you prospered to royal estate. Your renown went forth among the nations for your beauty; for it was perfect, through my majesty which I had put on you, says the Lord Yahweh. (Ezek. 16:3–14)

This passage first speaks of a neglected and unwanted child whom God takes as his own. A paternal nature of God is shown in the description of his clothing the child and saying, "You became mine." Later in the passage, more romantic imagery is drawn as God betroths and then marries the young woman. There is such tenderness in God that many of us have yet to discover.

The child is born unwanted and unloved; she is not only a Gentile but also a mongrel in the eyes of the Jews. There is nothing attractive or desirable about this child, and she is left to die. This was a form of infanticide. It is this unwanted and unloved child sentenced to death that God chooses to rescue. When no one else has compassion, God lovingly rescues this child. Thanks to God, the child grows up to be beautiful. For God it is not enough that he has rescued a mongrel orphan. As she grows he finds her mature and beautiful and enters into a covenant relationship with her. This child of humble origins is now married into royal blood. God dresses her in all sorts of finery to complement her natural beauty.

This is the greatest rags to riches story ever told. It is a fairy tale of love and redemption. This is a picture not only of God's relationship with Israel but also of his relationship with the church. We are the bride of Christ and we are truly loved.

Hosea's Love Story

Another story that conveys the romantic nature of God's love is that of Hosea and his wife, Gomer. Here's a summary of the story: God asks Hosea to find a prostitute and marry her. So Hosea marries Gomer, and they have children together. The children's names are prophetic statements of God's feelings toward Israel at that time—"not loved," "not my people." It comes as no surprise when Hosea's wife, being a prostitute, leaves him and returns to a promiscuous lifestyle. But God does not leave it there. He tells Hosea to find Gomer wherever she is and bring her back home.

The first thing that strikes me about this story is the kind of relationship that God and Hosea must have had for God to ask him to marry a prostitute and have children with her. It must have been one of love and obedience, because what God asked of Hosea could be asked only of someone who loved him and understood his purposes.

The main point I want to highlight in this story, however, is a description of God's covenant love toward Israel. Hosea's wife was a prostitute when he met and married her. Hosea had no illusions about the kind of woman she was but entered into covenant with her anyway. In the same way, God enters into a covenant relationship with us, even though we are undeserving of such love. The verse "While we were yet sinners, Christ died for us" (Rom. 5:8) captures the idea that God loved us not when we were righteous and good but while we were still steeped in sin.

When God asks Hosea to bring Gomer back, Hosea searches for his wayward wife. Imagine what it must have been like to have to go knocking on the doors of different men's houses, asking, "Hey, is my wife with you?" Yet the Scriptures show that God seeks *us* out even though we have been unfaithful. I see the Incarnation as a parallel to Hosea's seeking out Gomer. Christ came into the world to seek and save the lost. He came when we were undeserving. He came when we were not looking for him or desiring him. He came because he loved us so passionately that he was moved to action.

Our God is indeed a God of love. The Scriptures are full of statements and stories to back this up. We must not allow ourselves to perceive God as harsh, judgmental, and looking for an excuse to punish us. The psalmist says, "The LORD is gracious and compassionate, slow to anger and rich in love" (Ps. 145:8 NIV).

The Parable of the Lost Son

Another distinct picture of God is that of the loving Father who desires to be in good relationship with his children. In the parable of the lost son (Luke 15:11–32) God is depicted as a father who not only loves his son enough to allow him the freedom to make bad choices and mistakes, but also is willing to take the son back after he has made bad choices.

I have heard many sermons on this parable and am amazed by the variety of people's insights into this story. I recall one preacher explaining that in the story's time period and culture, for a son to ask his father for his inheritance would really imply that the son wished his father dead. In my view the son had no intention to return, so either way his relationship with his father would be over. Dead or alive. In the world we live in, many people would prefer that God did not exist; Nietzsche captured this mentality when he boldly declared, "God is dead." One of the main reasons people desire God to be dead is so that they, like the prodigal son, can carry on a life of wanton and destructive pleasure with no restraint whatsoever.

In the parable the father still loves his son and still desires a relationship with him despite all this. When this story is told or read properly with some dramatic impact, one cannot help but experience emotion as the son returns home. The father sees his son from a distance—which suggests that he was looking out for him—and then runs to his son, not like a father, but more like a little child running with abandon into the arms of his mummy. Before the son can deliver his well-rehearsed speech in full, the father has already accepted him, forgiven him, and begun pouring out his love upon him.

What a God we have that we can call him Father! Indeed he is our Father. By creation, by new birth, and by adoption, he is our Dad. He longs to pour out his love upon us and desires good things for us. He has given us the kind of free will that allows us to reject him and wish he no longer existed, but he still loves us.

At one point in my Christian life I was so mad at God that I wanted nothing to do with him. I was at university and was struggling with my faith because God seemed so distant. No matter what I said or did he seemed distant. I felt so abandoned by God that I became angry with him—so angry that I asked him, no begged him, to leave me alone. I remember saying to God that I knew he existed and that I even liked the guidance and wisdom for life in the Scriptures and was happy to obey them, but that I did not want to have a relationship with him.

Looking back on it, this was one of those times when I was glad that God does not answer all my prayers. God did not leave me alone. He was there. He was there when I finally found my way out of the desert in which I was lost. Then he brought me to a place where he lavished his love on me in a way that I had never known. Even though I had rejected him and almost wished he were dead, God did not stop loving me and caring for me. He was standing there with his arms wide open when I came to my senses and returned to him.

What a loving Father we have, full of loving affection and patient even with the most troublesome and stubborn children.

Attributes of Love

In Galatians 5:22–25 we find a description of the fruit of the Spirit that is very similar to the description of love in 1 Corinthians 13. This is because the "fruit of the Spirit" is another way to describe the fruit of the character of God.

> But the fruit of the Spirit is love, joy, peace, patience, kindness, goodness, faith, gentleness, and self-control. Against such things there is no law. Those who belong to Christ have crucified the flesh with its passions and lusts. If we live by the Spirit, let's also walk by the Spirit.

Christians have the Spirit within them, and the Spirit is God. As we walk in the power of the Spirit, we will display the character of the Spirit.

Galatians 2:20 says, "I have been crucified with Christ, and it is no longer I that live, but Christ living in me." The more I meditate on this verse, the more I realize that I really am a new creation, with Christ at the center of my life. If Christ is in me, then the character of Christ is in me. A struggle then ensues: will I allow Christ, with all his character attributes and power, to live out his holy life in me, or will I resist him by actively engaging in sinful acts?

The fruit of the Spirit are qualities that God possesses in abundance and wants to share with us. These qualities are the attributes of love and should inspire us to trust in God. He is indeed a good God who desires good things for his children and is not the great tyrant in the sky. Let me highlight a few things about Galatians 5:22–25 that add to what we saw in 1 Corinthians 13.

We may not often think of God as joyful, but more and more I realize that he is a God of joy. Only a God of joy could inspire Paul to write the book of Philippians, in which Paul, in the midst of much trial and difficulty, strongly encourages the Philippians to be joyful. If I were being persecuted for my faith and under house arrest, I don't think I would be feeling very joyful. Paul, however, was plugged into joy and contentment in God so that not only was he experiencing personal fulfillment (Phil. 4:12), but he was encouraging others to remain joyful too (Phil. 2:17–18). God is not in heaven in a bad mood and in a permanent state of anger with humankind. On the contrary, although God does get angry (at evil), he is also the Lord who "will rejoice over you with singing" (Zeph. 3:17).

The life of Jesus also points to a God full of joy. The psalmist writes prophetically of Jesus, "God, your God, has anointed you with the oil of gladness above your fellows" (Ps. 45:7). Jesus was a man who attracted people. I don't believe people would have followed him around if he had been a miserable kind of guy. The best people to measure the kind of person someone is are children. Children are amazing judges of character. Think about it. Have you ever seen children playing with someone who is miserable and grumpy? They are drawn to the people with a smile on their face and a sunny disposition. Jesus attracted children so much that the disciples tried to get rid of them, but he insisted they be allowed to come and blessed them (Matt. 19:13–15). People who take time to bless children stand to gain nothing from children. Often we are nice to others because of what we can get from them. Befriending children doesn't result in any material benefits or increased street cred, but you can enjoy the pure joy of their friendship and fun. God is a joyful and enjoyable God.

God is also self-controlled. This attribute of God is, I believe, why I have not yet been zapped by God. The Bible says God cannot be tempted (James 1:13). In his life on earth Jesus was tempted, but because of his self-control he did not yield to sin. Jesus did not just lose his temper; he had a righteous anger sometimes, but all his actions were calculated and not simply emotional responses to the circumstances. The idea of God's self-control should be very comforting to us. We can know that his actions in history that are difficult to understand are part of a loving master plan and not thoughtless responses to unforeseen and uncontrollable circumstances. We have a God we can rely on to think through his every action—because getting perspective on a situation is not difficult for an all-knowing God.

Compassionate Love

I am also struck by the compassion of God. "The Lord is gracious and compassionate, slow to anger and rich in love (Ps. 145:8 NIV). God's compassion comes through on many levels. Jesus, for example, clearly displayed compassion for the widows and orphans and care for the needs of people. His feeding of the five thousand was an act of compassion. He healed the sick out of compassion. *Compassion* is a hard word to define, but in essence it is caring about the suffering of others and desiring to help them find relief. Real love is always accompanied by compassion. It has been said that the opposite of love is not hate but indifference. If we are people who love, we will not be indifferent to the needs of others.

I am bothered when people make God out to be indifferent. People talk about God being the author of suffering in the world when the truth is that the suffering in the world grieves

God more than it grieves us. It grieves him so much that he has intervened and provided a way for us to find some relief from suffering, both in this life and the next. A compassionate God does not stand by and watch while the world self-destructs. He acts and moves and makes a difference. A compassionate God does not take any delight in watching people burn in hell. He sent his Son so that none need perish.

God does not delight in evil but rejoices in truth. Because of his compassion he is involved in our lives. The Holy Spirit draws alongside us and helps us in our time of need. Jesus intercedes for us before God because he cares.

Irresistible Love

Why would we exchange a holy, righteous, and merciful God for a tyrant in the sky? One reason people preach about a tyrant is that fear is an effective tool for controlling people. Scaring people might keep people in line, but it obscures the true nature of God. When people are scared of God and dare not approach him, they are less likely to discover the truth about him and his commands. We don't seem to realize that God himself has chosen the route of love to win our hearts and establish his kingdom.

The Jews were waiting for a Messiah who would fight and kill and put an end to the Roman occupation. Instead what they got was a loving, friendly carpenter who was too busy healing the sick and casting out demons to be caught up in any political manipulation and violence. Do we, like the Jews, prefer so much to create our own picture of the Messiah that we miss the reality of who God is? Would we rather have the tiger that slays instead of the Lamb that was slain?

UP

DOWN

IN

OUT

up

DOWN

IN

OUT

God is calling us to an intimate relationship with him. It is an offer that we should not turn down. To enter into this relationship we need to trust that God is truly good and not just taking us for the biggest ride ever. If we do not know who God really is, then we need to make knowing him a priority. I boldly challenge anyone: if you get to know God through the Scriptures and the power of the Spirit, you will not be able to resist falling in love with him. His love is irresistible.

G race, grace, grace. The theme of his talk was unmistakable. I cannot remember much detail of what he spoke about that night, but I remember this: he talked about grace.

The well-known speaker and author George Verwer had come to speak at our Christian Union. For me George is a real role model. He played a significant role in establishing Operation Mobilization (OM). My first encounter with the work of OM was when I was a child in primary school, living in Sierra Leone. Our whole school, along with many other schools from our city, had taken a trip to the OM ship to experience this floating library that went all over the world. So here was the famous founder of OM at my university Christian Union. Many Christians from the area came to hear George's pearls of wisdom.

During his talk, George repeatedly encouraged us to read a book by Charles Swindoll called *The Grace Awakening*. At the end of the meeting I was one of the first people to get to the bookstall at the back to get a copy of this book. Unfortunately no copies were available. There was, however, another book called *The Ragamuffin Gospel* which George said communicated a similar message. That day I not only bought that book, but because I was an avid reader and George likes to give books away, I ended up with a load of books and also CDs and teaching tapes. I made it a priority to get hold of *The Grace Awakening* but was content to delve into *The Ragamuffin Gospel* in the meantime. I took the book home and started to read.

First Encounter

Reading *The Ragamuffin Gospel* was my first conscious encounter with grace. There was much in the book that I did not grasp, but the little I was getting had an impact on me. I read of a God who was so loving and accepting that he was willing to forgive the most hardened sinner. Like a man jilted and betrayed by his lover over and over again, God was willing to take people back no matter how many times they failed. Brennan Manning, the book's author, was a Catholic priest who had struggled with alcoholism and had experienced God's forgiveness and restoration. God's grace had been sufficient. Grace, I learned, is for those who recognize that they need it, and I needed it. Let me share a bit of my story.

I made an initial commitment to Christ in Sierra Leone and later found myself in a boarding school just outside London feeling very alone and sad. Trying hard to make friends, I began doing the same things as my peers and soon found myself sliding down the slippery slope of a teenage life that included drinking, smoking, and partying hard. There is no need to describe all the trouble I got into, but I will say that this point marked the start of an awful cycle that lasted several years.

The cycle went like this: I would be getting on okay in my Christian life but then would start to backslide and get into all kinds of trouble. Eventually I would hit a crisis where I was either so scared of what God might do to me or in such desperate need of his help that I would return to him. I then would find myself at the front of a meeting recommitting my life to God. I repeated this cycle several times over a few years. Although I was choosing to walk with God, I was ashamed of the things I had done in my wandering state. I felt inadequate and unworthy and unfit for use by the Master. All this meant that I was ready to hear the message of grace in *The Ragamuffin Gospel*. As I read how Manning had found God's forgiveness, I had hope of finding this forgiveness myself.

The Amazing Part about Grace

It was no coincidence that not much later I read another book about grace—Philip Yancey's *What's So Amazing About Grace?* I was again confronted with a truth so profound that I could not ignore it. The book told me that God loves me no matter what, that God's love is unconditional, and that even though I had backslidden many times, this was not a problem for God. God, I was realizing, was always ready to give me a fresh start. But this was too much for me to take in all at once.

I had carried guilt around for years. I saw myself as a second-class Christian compared to those who had walked a steady path their whole Christian life. For so long I had tried to live a good Christian life out of fear of punishment, and now I was hearing that I did not need to be afraid. The thought that the almighty God would still love me even if I messed up was almost unimaginable.

It was then that scriptures such as Romans 8:35–39 started to make sense to me:

UP

DOWN

IN

OUT

Who shall separate us from the love of Christ? Could oppression, or anguish, or persecution, or famine, or nakedness, or peril, or sword? Even as it is written, "For your sake we are killed all day long. We were accounted as sheep for the slaughter." No, in all these things, we are more than conquerors through him who loved us. For I am persuaded, that neither death, nor life, nor angels, nor principalities, nor things present, nor things to come, nor powers, nor height, nor depth, nor any other created thing, will be able to separate us from the love of God, which is in Christ Jesus our Lord.

Even though I had read this scripture many times, in my head I thought God would love me only if I were good. This was my experience with people, and I applied this thinking to God. Much of the love that people offer is conditional; they make statements such as "If you love me, you will..." or "If you..., I will be your friend." As a result, many of us are conditioned from a young age to believe that love is conditional and that acceptance is dependent on behavior.

When I discipline my children, I make an extra point to hug them afterward. This has produced discipline without rejection, so that now, even when I have disciplined them, they will come to me for comfort because they know that I still love and accept them. I learned this form of discipline from God. In my relationship with him, he has loved me unconditionally. Even when he has put me through hard times, he has not stopped loving me. Before I grasped this, however, I had associated God's discipline with his rejection, because of what I observed in society.

I believe that many people live their lives and make choices out of a desire to be loved and accepted. The young boy who starts smoking just to get in with the cool crowd does this out of a desire to be accepted. The teenage girl who sleeps with her boyfriend does this out of fear that he will break up with her and she will end up alone and unloved. The businessman who stays late at work to impress the bosses does this because he loves the attention he gets for being such a high achiever. The list goes on.

It is greatly comforting to know that God's discipline is a sign not of his rejection but of his love. The mind-blowing revelation that I do not have to earn God's love and that nothing can separate me from God's unconditional love in Christ has transformed my Christian walk. The fact that the almighty God, who created the universe and everything within it, loves and accepts me is a truth that still causes my heart to miss a beat and my knees to go weak. That God loves me unconditionally and that I don't have to earn this love takes my breath away.

Grace Is an Aspect of Love

God's grace is an aspect of his love and can be expressed in three ways:

- His unconditional love and acceptance of me regardless of my past, present, or future
- His desire to forgive even my worst sins no matter how many times I commit them
- His pleasure toward me regardless of what I do or don't do—I do not have to perform for him

Many people don't like the idea that God will accept anyone, that he will forgive any sin, and that we do not have to perform for him to accept and love us. They believe that preaching this

UP

DOWN

IN

OUT

kind of grace is unhelpful and open to abuse. I appreciate that it can be open to abuse, but the preaching of this kind of grace is essential to convey the love of God and the good news of the gospel. The truth is that real grace is very much open to abuse, and anyone who preaches a grace that cannot be abused is not really preaching grace.

In an age when people sign prenuptial agreements, it is hard to believe that someone would commit to love someone regardless of the cost. Imagine a multimillionaire who falls in love with a young homeless woman and they decide to get married. Everyone around the man warns him, "She is only marrying you for your money." But he loves her and wants to marry her. His lawyers strongly suggest that he write up a prenuptial agreement; however, the man feels this is unnecessary. He loves the woman and wants to share everything with her. So not only does he decide to marry her with no prenuptial agreement, but he also gives her a Platinum American Express card on the wedding day. In reality the man is leaving himself wide open to losing everything. His new wife could easily abuse his love and trust, but that is a risk he is willing to take because he loves her.

During the marriage there are times when the man's wife spends more money on the card than he would desire, but he carries on loving her. There are also times when she is unfaithful to him, but he still loves her and does not withdraw credit card privileges. Now imagine that the man's wife divorces him, takes half his money, and spends it all on wild living. Should he keep loving her? Should he take her back if she decides to return? Well imagine that he does take her back. This story is beginning to sound a lot like the parable of the lost son.

God's grace is so good that it can be abused, and that is God's intention. Not that it be abused, but that it is so good that it *can* be abused. A love with conditions attached is not love but a contract. Grace with limits is not grace but a cheap imitation of grace.

Obedience from Love

In my experience, God's grace does not inspire abuse; rather, it inspires genuine devotion, dedication, and obedience. This was one of the first things that I noticed after God revealed his grace to me: instead of wanting to take grace as a license to sin, I was inspired to obedience. How did this happen?

First, in realizing how much God loves me, I also realized that someone who loves me enough to die for me and leave himself so vulnerable was someone who meant me no harm. It is a real paradigm shift to move from the idea that God is waiting to punish you for making a mistake to the idea that God wants the best for you and wants to give you a full and complete life. As I grasped this idea that God wants to help me live life to the full, I recognized that obedience is for my own good. God is not a killjoy trying to put a damper on my life, but actually the opposite.

Some of the scary things that we read in the Bible about judgment and punishment are not God's threats but are simply his telling us the truth. Winkie Pratney once said, "God's laws are descriptions of reality." God tells us the truth about the way the universe works. For example, the Bible says that "the wages of sin is death." I used to interpret this as: if you sin, God will punish you with death. But now I see that this is just a fact: the effect that sin has on our lives is eventual death.

Imagine this. A man is walking along a coastal path in southern Scotland. The path has a fence on either side. On one side there is a farm, and on the other side is a 500-foot sheer drop onto rocks. Along the way the man sees two signs. On the fence of the farm, a notice reads, "PRIVATE LAND. Trespassers will be shot and killed on sight." On the opposite fence the local council have put up a sign that says, "DANGER! Sheer drop. If you cross this fence, you will likely fall off the cliff and die." Both signs warn of an end result of death, but for different reasons. In the case of the farm, death results from punishment; but in the case of the cliff, death results from gravity. The law of gravity is not a punishment but a reality. It is a fact that if you fall 500 feet onto rocks, you will probably die.

Obedience came much more easily once I understood that God's laws exist to protect me because God loves me.

The second reason I was inspired to obedience is that God, I learned, is displeased and even hurt by sin and disobedience, probably because he hates watching us wreck our lives. Genesis 6:5–6 says, "The LORD saw how great man's wickedness on the earth had become…and his heart was filled with pain" (NIV). As someone in a love relationship with God, I want to cause him as little pain as possible. In the same way that husband and wife or father and son do not want to hurt each other, I am slowly learning not to do things that will hurt God—not out of a fear of punishment but out of a genuine desire not to hurt him.

Old Testament Grace

The concept of grace is not restricted to the New Testament but is apparent in God's relationship with Israel in the Old Testament. I once heard someone say that mercy is when we don't get what we deserve (punishment) and grace is when we get what we don't deserve (blessings and forgiveness). In God's dealings with Israel, the people received many favors that arguably they did not deserve.

The Hebrew word *chesed* is often translated "lovingkindness." Together the words *loving* and *kindness* communicate the heart of the meaning of *chesed* but are still somewhat limited. Scholars say that *chesed* entails much more than love and kindness; it entails God's covenant love for Israel.

In our day and culture we do not experience or value covenant in the same way that many ancient cultures did. A covenant was a binding contract between two parties, and the seal of the covenant was blood. Sometimes the parties exchanged vows declaring the death of a party that broke the covenant.

God made a covenant with Israel that he would be their God. He promised to love them unconditionally and never forsake them. He faithfully kept all his promises to Israel, and he continues to be faithful to those who have a relationship with him through Jesus. God's covenant love is not dependent on us or our behavior but is solely dependent on him. His word is a bond.

New Testament Grace

In the New Testament, "grace" is translated from the Greek word *charis*, which can mean a gift of sorts. A friend from Greece helped me understand the word. She said that *charis* is when you give someone a gift, something that you own, that the person could never get for himself or herself. For example, if you give someone the gift of your love, that is something that the recipient cannot walk into a shop and buy. Or if a millionaire gives a poor person a rare and expensive diamond ring, that is something the poor person could not afford. A *charis* gift is therefore

UP

DOWN

IN

OUT

up

something that you cannot get on two levels: either you cannot afford it or it is priceless.

God has given us the gift of his Son. There is no way to put a price on Jesus. He is a gift that we could not demand or earn. We could not have forced Jesus to give up his own life; he gave it up of his own free will.

We can face challenges today in our application of grace when we encounter questions such as whether we are still required to obey the law or whether we are now free from the law and living under grace. This is where the legalism versus license debate surfaces, and it seems that some people quickly forget that it is "by grace [we] have been saved through faith, and that not of [ourselves]; it is the gift of God" (Eph. 2:8).

DOWN

In Galatians Paul strongly rebukes the church because although they began their faith walking by grace, they turned to religious legalism in an effort to keep their salvation. Some people today believe that rules and regulations keep people from falling away. Although they may mean well, these people have missed the point.

IN

At this point I enter controversial ground, but there is a need to challenge some popular but errant Christian thinking. Paul says in Galatians that we who are led by the Spirit are no longer under the law (Gal. 5:18) and are not bound to obey any Old Testament laws. He points out that if we want to obey one law, then we should obey them all (Gal. 5:3).

OUT

I have heard people object to tattoos by citing Old Testament laws as prooftexts. Some people have rules about what to eat based on the Levitical diet, but the New Testament teaches that all food is appropriate to eat (Mark 7:19; Rom. 14:20). Many of our churches strictly and passionately teach the principle of tithing, but this principle is based almost exclusively on the Old

Testament book of Malachi. The New Testament teaches the
principle not of tithing but of generosity. There is a freedom
that goes with generosity. There is, of course, also a responsibility that goes with it, and such personal responsibility is what
people sometimes try to avoid by instead opting for rules and
regulations. In my opinion it is easy to have a fixed law about
how we give instead of responding to each situation in prayerful
giving.

Grace means that we no longer need to be prisoners of rules
and regulations. Only one law remains for us: the command to
love God and others. Paul felt so strongly about this issue that
he rebuked Peter (Gal. 2:11–14), even though Peter had walked
with Christ and was a senior leader. And Paul did not quietly
pull Peter to the side to challenge him; he rebuked him publicly,
because grace was such an important issue. We must not forget
that works cannot and never will save us from our sins.

Falling from Grace

You may think that I am being condemning and judgmental
toward those in legalism. On the contrary, I have compassion for
those who are enslaved by legalism, because I myself have had
similar struggles. The problem is that we are always looking for
ways to make ourselves feel better than others. Self-righteousness
is the feeling of being righteous apart from Christ's work on the
Cross, and legalism fits the bill perfectly when it comes to breed-
ing self-righteousness.

I was once in a situation where I allowed the enemy to
deceive me into legalism. I was being blessed greatly by a wonderful Bible teacher. However, there were some things in the
teacher's more personal sharing that I took to heart in a way that

led me to become very religious in my approach to righteousness. What the Lord meant to be for good, the enemy took as an opportunity to enslave me once again. I embraced a measure of asceticism that involved things like a change of diet, a ban on watching movies (one of my favorite hobbies), and other petty religious things.

This might sound silly to you, and it does to me now, but at the time it seemed to make sense. (We all know that some of this stuff, like certain movies and foods, is bad for us anyway.) For a few months I stuck to this new strict lifestyle. The truth is, I felt quite good about myself and looked down on those who were "enslaved" by things such as movies, parties, and chocolate. By observing these self-imposed laws, I felt like a better Christian.

One day God challenged me about what I was doing, and the words "Foolish Olu, who has bewitched you?" went through my mind. Galatians 3:1–5 says:

Foolish Galatians, who has bewitched you not to obey the truth, before whose eyes Jesus Christ was openly set forth among you as crucified? I just want to learn this from you. Did you receive the Spirit by the works of the law, or by hearing of faith? Are you so foolish? Having begun in the Spirit, are you now completed in the flesh? Did you suffer so many things in vain, if it is indeed in vain? He therefore who supplies the Spirit to you, and works miracles among you, does he do it by the works of the law, or by hearing of faith?

I was cut to the quick. I realized that I had fallen from grace. "You are alienated from Christ, you who desire to be justified by the law. You have fallen away from grace" (Gal. 5:4). I who had boldly preached the good news of grace had become a paid-up member of the legalists club. I was so deeply grieved that I entered into some serious repentance. Even now as I think back, tears start to gather in my eyes. To think that I could fall away from God's grace that had been so wonderfully revealed to me! We are all vulnerable to falling into legalism. Legalism is just as dangerous, if not more dangerous, than license, because legalism breeds pride and security in the wrong thing. I have never met a backslider who was proud of what he or she was doing. So then, as Paul asks, "Shall we continue in sin, that grace may abound?" (Rom. 6:1). The answer is a resounding no. But in some ways those who are operating in license are more dependent on God's grace than those who are legalistic and depend on their own good works. We must be vigilant to reject any gospel that is a different gospel from that of salvation by grace.

Grace to Others

Grace has the ability to transform us in a way that not only sets us free from legalism but also enables us to be a blessing to others and fill their lives with grace. Walking in grace means that in the same way that God accepts us, we ought to accept one another.

Philip Yancey tells this short story in *What's So Amazing About Grace?* A promiscuous woman was struggling with life because of her lifestyle. She was looking for help. In a conversation someone suggested that she go to a local church to inquire about help. The woman's reply was, "Why would I do that? I feel bad enough about myself already."

The church of Jesus Christ has gained a reputation of being ungracious, judgmental, and not accepting. Someone described the church as the only group that shoots its wounded. How can it be that the ambassadors of Christ can be so un-Christlike?

Jesus was the epitome of grace. He prevented the stoning of an adulteress. He let a prostitute wipe his feet with her hair. He spent so much time with sinners that he was accused of being a winebibber and a glutton. Indeed, he befriended sinners so much that even today people make up stories about him being secretly married to Mary Magdalene, who some believe was a prostitute. Jesus loved sinners so much that he died for them.

We are called to love as Jesus loved. We are called to show grace to others as Christ has shown grace to us. In the same way that the Bible says to love your neighbor as yourself, I would also say to show grace to others as you show grace to yourself. This might sound simple enough, but many people don't even show grace to themselves. They punish themselves and live guilt-ridden lives even though Christ has forgiven them. If you can relate to this description, my prayer is that you would learn how to receive God's grace through faith. Until you have learned to receive grace for yourself, you will struggle to show grace to others.

On the other hand, some people, though they excuse themselves, are harsh with others. One of my mentors said that we judge ourselves by our intentions but we judge others by their actions. It is all too easy to judge others without thinking about the intentions of their hearts.

God has called us to be people who live grace-filled lives through faith in his Son. This grace is available to us and, as Christ said to Paul, sufficient for us (2 Cor. 12:9). Attempting to live the Christian life without walking in the grace of God will only end in pain and disappointment. We live in a world where people are desperate for grace and acceptance, and that includes us. We need to be channels of God's grace. As we receive God's grace, we must pour it out to a broken and needy world.

UP

DOWN

IN

OUT

UP ———————— **3. Intimacy with God**

DOWN

IN

OUT

W*hy am I a Christian?* This is a question that many of us ask ourselves at various points in our Christian walk.

My initial response to the question was that I was a Christian to escape the wrath of God, so that I would find myself in heaven when that dreaded day came. My attitude at that time was: "I am a Christian now. I am going to heaven, so I'm sorted. Now, back to living my life just as I've always lived it." Later I realized that there was more to being a Christian, and I decided that the purpose of being a Christian was to serve God. As noble an endeavour as serving God might be, it still misses the mark and can lead to a works approach to the Christian life.

A better and more fundamental question than, why am I a Christian? is, why did Jesus die? It is wise to go to the Bible to answer this question. John 3:16 states, "For God so loved the world, that he gave his one and only Son, that whoever believes in him should not perish, but have eternal life." Before, my understanding of this scripture was simply that Jesus died so that I would not go to hell but live forever. It naturally followed that when I shared the gospel, my goal was to get people "saved" (the "eternal life" part of John 3:16).

Although it is true that eternal salvation is part of the gospel, a salvation-only approach to spreading the gospel falls short of what I believe God's purposes are for us. The salvation experience is like arriving at the airport of a holiday destination—there is still a whole lot more to a holiday than arriving. With that in mind, John 3:16 tells us more than we may realize.

Beyond Salvation

I am obsessed with the meaning of words. In our postmodern age, one word can have many different meanings depending on what you are talking about or who you are talking to. I recall when some people used the words *wicked* and *bad* to mean "good."

The Bible is kind enough to provide the definition of certain words and phrases so that we can understand what they mean when we come across them in a text. So my question is, what does *eternal life* mean in the Bible? John 17:3 says, "This is eternal life, that they should know you, the only true God, and him whom you sent, Jesus Christ." The Greek word for "know," *ginosko,* expresses deep intimacy and can be used to describe sexual intimacy. I am not about to suggest that Jesus died so that we might have sexual intimacy with God, but I do want to suggest that Jesus died not merely to save us from hell but to bring us into close fellowship with God.

At the risk of challenging many years of tradition, I believe that we are misguided when we preach a gospel of salvation from sin. God's path to restore relationship with his creation was to deal with the problem of sin. But the real good news is

UP

DOWN

IN

OUT

not simply that sin has been dealt with but that we can have the kind of fellowship with God that even goes beyond what Adam and Eve lost in the Garden of Eden.

Allow me to explore the story we call "the fall of man" from a slightly different angle. In the Garden of Eden, Adam and Eve walked with God in great closeness. Adam was so close to God that he was granted the privilege of naming God's creatures. The first thing Adam and Eve did after they disobeyed God was hide from his presence: "They heard the voice of Yahweh God walking in the garden in the cool of the day, and the man and his wife hid themselves from the presence of Yahweh God among the trees of the garden" (Gen. 3:8). An immediate result of their sin was that they could no longer handle the presence of God and therefore no longer be intimate with God. (It's not possible to be intimate with someone if you can't even stand that person's presence.) Then, as a further result, Adam and Eve were thrown out of the Garden of Eden and denied not only close fellowship with God but also access to the Tree of Life.

The end result of Adam and Eve's disobedience was that the human race was denied the privilege of an eternity of intimacy with God. At best, people could hope for a lifetime of significantly limited fellowship with God.

Then comes the Cross. Christ's work on the Cross was to restore the broken relationship between God and humanity by removing sin. And now, because sin has been removed as a barrier, we have access not only to God but also to his life-giving power that strengthens and restores us in this life and will sustain us for eternity.

Second Corinthians 5:18–21 provides a compelling description of the work of Jesus:

But all things are of God, who reconciled us to himself through Jesus Christ, and gave to us the ministry of reconciliation; namely, that God was in Christ reconciling the world to himself, not reckoning to them their trespasses, and having committed to us the word of reconciliation. We are therefore ambassadors on behalf of Christ, as though God were entreating by us: we beg you on behalf of Christ, be reconciled to God. For him who knew no sin he made to be sin on our behalf; so that in him we might become the righteousness of God.

As the work of Christ was (and is) to restore humanity's relationship with God, the work of Christians is to plead with the world to be reconciled to God on behalf of Christ.

Missing the Point

There is always a danger that we might ignore such a simple truth and trap ourselves in all kinds of religious activities. Many times we measure people's faith by external factors such as church attendance, Bible knowledge, and public prayer. The true measure of Christian faith, however, is a person's knowledge of God in Christ. Paul warns us not to lose the simplicity of the Christian faith. "But I am afraid that somehow, as the serpent deceived Eve in his craftiness, so your minds might be corrupted from the simplicity that is in Christ" (2 Cor. 11:3). It is entirely possible to be involved in the things that point to Jesus but still miss *him*. Jesus himself pointed this out to the Pharisees: "You search the Scriptures, because you think that in them you have eternal life; and these are they which testify about me. Yet you will not come to me, that you may have life" (John 5:39–40).

Many of us get caught up in doing noble things, such as missions work, preaching, or caring for the needy, but the point of Christianity is to get as close as we can to a person, or even three persons. I am referring here to the Godhead, not polytheism. Eternal life is about an intimate and personal knowledge of God. It is about knowing the Father, the Son whom the Father sent, and the Spirit who dwells with us. We will not find life anywhere else but within the persons of the Trinity. We may be great Bible scholars or may even work miracles, but if we do not know Christ, we have missed the point. In short, being a Christian is about knowing God, not just knowing about him.

> Not everyone who says to me, "Lord, Lord," will enter into the Kingdom of Heaven; but he who does the will of my Father who is in heaven. Many will tell me in that day, "Lord, Lord, didn't we prophesy in your name, in your name cast out demons, and in your name do many mighty works?" Then I will tell them, "I never knew you. Depart from me, you who work iniquity." (Matt. 7:21–23)

It is our personal knowledge of Jesus, and the obedience birthed from it, that will determine whether we enter into eternal life.

A Love Beyond Knowledge

One of my favorite sections of Scripture is found in Ephesians:

> For this cause, I bow my knees to the Father of our Lord Jesus Christ, from whom every family in heaven and on earth is named, that he would grant you, according to the

riches of his glory, that you may be strengthened with power through his Spirit in the inward man; that Christ may dwell in your hearts through faith; to the end that you, being rooted and grounded in love, may be strengthened to comprehend with all the saints what is the breadth and length and height and depth, and to know Christ's love which surpasses knowledge, that you may be filled with all the fullness of God. (Eph. 3:14–19)

This passage is powerful and speaks to us about the foundation of our faith. At the risk of sounding formulaic, I believe it shows us that the key to being filled with the fullness of God lies in one's ability to grasp his love. You cannot grasp God's love outside of an intimate relationship with him. To say it in the reverse, an intimate relationship is characterized by love. You cannot talk about intimacy without talking about love.

Verse 19 says that we can "know Christ's love which surpasses knowledge." The word translated "know" is the same word (*ginosko*) that we saw earlier in John 17:3. The word translated "knowledge" comes from the Greek *gnosis,* which is connected to the word *science* (*gnosis* is translated as *scientia* in Latin). *Gnosis* is an intellectual kind of knowledge. Ultimately this verse is saying that we can know the love of Christ in an intimate, experiential way that goes beyond mere intellectual assent to the idea that God loves us. The only way to experience love beyond the intellectual and theoretical forms that many people talk about is to be in an intimate relationship.

The promise is that when we know this love, we will be filled with all the fullness of God (Eph. 3:19). Stop and meditate on what it means to be filled with the fullness of God. Neither I nor anyone completely knows what being filled with the fullness

UP

DOWN

IN

OUT

of God means, but I am excited at the prospect of being filled with it through a loving relationship with Jesus.

Our Reward: Knowing God

Often when people talk about heaven, they focus on rewards and objects, such as mansions and streets of gold, but I believe that God has a greater treasure that awaits us in the life to come. In Genesis 15:1 God says something significant to Abraham: "After these things the word of Yahweh came to Abram in a vision, saying, 'Don't be afraid, Abram. I am your shield, your exceedingly great reward.'" The great reward that Abraham experienced was God himself. If you think about it, the most valuable entity in existence is God. The treasure that we are invited to obtain for ourselves is the pleasure of knowing God. This makes sense of the idea of hell: those who have chosen not to have fellowship with God in this life will obviously not be worthy of receiving God as their reward in the life to come; therefore, an eternity apart from the Life Giver awaits them.

Matthew 13 has an interesting description of the kingdom of heaven: "Again, the Kingdom of Heaven is like a man who is a merchant seeking fine pearls, who having found one pearl of great price, he went and sold all that he had, and bought it" (Matt. 13:45–46). I believe that God himself is the pearl of great price that we are called to sacrifice all to obtain. No kingdom is greater than its king. As valuable and precious as the kingdom of God is, it does not surpass the Creator in its greatness.

Jeremiah 9:23–24 further emphasizes the importance of knowing God. Although the Bible usually discourages all kinds of boasting, this passage makes an exception to the rule.

Thus says Yahweh, Don't let the wise man glory in his wisdom, neither let the mighty man glory in his might, don't let the rich man glory in his riches; but let him who glories glory in this, that he has understanding, and knows me, that I am Yahweh who exercises loving kindness, justice, and righteousness, in the earth: for in these things I delight, says Yahweh.

God allows Christians to boast that they know him and understand him. This highlights the importance that God places on knowing him. We can get to know God only if we take the time to develop a relationship with him. God calls us to a place of knowing him as the one who exercises lovingkindness, justice, and righteousness. We cannot know and experience these things from God without having an intimate relationship with him.

Friends of God

God has placed examples in the Bible of men and women who made knowing God and having a relationship with him a priority in their lives. One of the first people we encounter who walked with God is Enoch. "Enoch walked with God after he became the father of Methuselah three hundred years, and became the father of sons and daughters" (Gen. 5:22). This verse tells us when Enoch began his walk with God and how long it lasted. Then the verse that puzzles us all. "Enoch walked with God, and he was not, for God took him" (Gen. 5:24). It seems that after Enoch had a very long relationship with God, God took Enoch to himself. "By faith, Enoch was taken away, so that he wouldn't see death, and he was not found, because God translated him. For he has had testimony given to him that before his

59

UP

DOWN

IN

OUT

translation he had been well pleasing to God" (Heb. 11:5). What if we all walked so closely with God that we did not die but God simply took us to himself? We might not all be Enoch who was taken up, but we certainly can walk closely with God.

Another example of someone in close relationship with God is Abraham, who is described as a friend of God. "And the Scripture was fulfilled which says, 'Abraham believed God, and it was accounted to him as righteousness;' and he was called the friend of God" (James 2:23). Imagine what it would be like to be called the friend of God. Not merely an acquaintance or a servant, but a friend. It is an incredible privilege to be called the friend of God.

The key to cultivating a friendship with God is making time for him, time in which we can sit in his presence and enjoy fellowship with him through things like worship, prayer, and Bible reading. In the New Testament, Mary is someone who cultivated such a relationship. Jesus had a close relationship with Mary and her sister Martha (see John 11:5). Luke writes about how Mary prioritized time sitting at Jesus' feet and Jesus affirmed her choice even though her sister was frustrated that she was not helping out (Luke 10:38–42).

The individual who stands out to me the most as having an intimate relationship with God is Moses. "Yahweh spoke to Moses face to face, as a man speaks to his friend" (Exod. 33:11). Imagine God visiting you regularly and speaking to you. Moses had such an intimate friendship with God that he was able to avert the destruction of Israel by persuading his Friend to hold back his wrath. In this story Moses goes up the mountain (Exod. 24:15) to meet with God and receive the Ten Commandments. Because Moses is gone a long time and the people don't really know what is happening, they decide to make a calf out of gold and worship it. The people's blatant idolatry makes God angry, and in his wrath he declares that he will wipe out the nation and start again with Moses. "Yahweh said to Moses, 'I have seen these people, and behold, they are a stiff-necked people. Now therefore leave me alone, that my wrath may burn hot against them, and that I may consume them; and I will make of you a great nation'" (Exod. 32:9–10). Moses, however, persuades God not to wipe the people out, and God changes his mind. "Yahweh repented of the evil which he said he would do to his people" (Exod. 32:14).

I believe that Moses was able to change God's mind because of his relationship with God. There are valuable lessons to learn from this passage about the connection between prayer and relationship with God. The passage indicates that God truly responds to the prayers of his friends. My heart's desire is that I would become the kind of friend that God listens to.

The New Testament also has examples of friendship with God. I am particularly jealous of the apostle John. I think of John as the love apostle. He highlights the importance of love and relationship not only in his letters but also in his behavior, which we see in his written account of the life of Jesus. John shamelessly describes himself as "the disciple whom Jesus loved" (see John 13:23; 19:26; 20:2; 21:7; 21:20). This phrase reveals that, for John, the fact that Jesus loved him was so important that he wanted it to be part of his identity. John was one of the three disciples who made up Jesus' inner circle that he took with him to the mount of transfiguration (Mark 9:2). He had such a close and intimate relationship with Jesus that he quite happily laid his head on Jesus' chest at the meal table: "One of his disciples, whom Jesus loved, was at the table, leaning against Jesus' breast" (John 13:23). Such affection cannot go unnoticed.

John's passion and love for Jesus can be an inspirational example to us all.

Interpreting the Scriptures

Some might say that I have been reading too much into the Scriptures. Some might even say that people are affectionate with God because of human nature but that God does not relate to humanity in affectionate terms. However, many Bible scholars see the Song of Solomon as an allegory for the relationship God desires to have with his church. If the book is indeed inspired by God (and I believe it is), then God is obviously not shy about romance. The Song uses very intimate language about the lover and the beloved, and regardless of whether you think the lover is King Solomon or the shepherd, I think you will agree on one thing: if this story represents anything of Christ's desire for his bride, then it is clear that God does relate to humanity in affectionate terms and does desire to have a certain level of intimacy with us.

The love story in the book of Hosea (discussed in chapter 1) is even more clear than the Song of Solomon, because God himself uses Hosea's relationship with his wife to parallel his relationship with Israel. In short, God casts himself in the role of the abandoned husband desiring a renewed intimacy with his unfaithful wife.

In the New Testament Paul contributes to our understanding of God's affection by adding a few thoughts about Christ and the church:

> Wives, be subject to your own husbands, as to the Lord. For the husband is the head of the wife, and Christ also is the head of the assembly, being himself the savior of the body.

But as the assembly is subject to Christ, so let the wives also be to their own husbands in everything. Husbands, love your wives, even as Christ also loved the assembly, and gave himself up for it; that he might sanctify it, having cleansed it by the washing of water with the word, that he might present the assembly to himself gloriously, not having spot or wrinkle or any such thing; but that it should be holy and without blemish. Even so husbands also ought to love their own wives as their own bodies. He who loves his own wife loves himself. For no man ever hated his own flesh; but nourishes and cherishes it, even as the Lord also does the assembly; because we are members of his body, of his flesh and bones. "For this cause a man will leave his father and mother, and will be joined to his wife. The two will become one flesh." This mystery is great, but I speak concerning Christ and of the assembly. Nevertheless each of you must also love his own wife even as himself; and let the wife see that she respects her husband. (Eph. 5:22–33)

In this passage Paul speaks of a great mystery where the relationship between a husband and wife is symbolic of the relationship between Christ and the church. In most cultures the highest form of intimate relationship between two people is the marriage covenant. The use of marriage as a symbol of Christ relating to his church speaks not only of the intimacy but also of the exclusivity of this relationship.

Conditions for Real Intimacy

Intimacy with God is a privilege, not a right. It is reserved for those who have entered into a life-giving covenant with God and have an ongoing walk with him characterized by obedience. The conversion experience is only the starting point of the relationship. As we preach the good news, we are extending an invitation to all creation that it can enter into an intimate relationship with God. Once someone has experienced conversion, the level of intimacy that that person experiences will depend on his or her willingness to obey. Matthew points out that those whom Christ will allow into the kingdom are those who do the will of the Father: "Not everyone who says to me, 'Lord, Lord,' will enter into the Kingdom of Heaven; but he who does the will of my Father who is in heaven" (Matt. 7:21).

My experiences have taught me that growth in our relationship with God will not occur without obedience. Imagine that you had a friend who ignored everything you said, even when you were trying to give advice. That would not make for a good relationship. In the same way we cannot expect to disobey God and yet grow close to him. Jesus, quoting Isaiah, communicates this principle:

> He answered them, "Why do you also disobey the commandment of God because of your tradition? For God commanded, 'Honor your father and your mother,' and, 'He who speaks evil of father or mother, let him be put to death.' But you say, 'Whoever may tell his father or his mother, "Whatever help you might otherwise have gotten from me is a gift devoted to God," he shall not honor his father or mother.' You have made the commandment of God void because of your tradition. You hypocrites! Well did Isaiah prophesy of you, saying, 'These people draw near to me with their mouth, and honor me with their lips; but their heart is far from me. And in vain do they worship me, teaching as doctrine rules made by men.'" (Matt. 15:3–9)

Those who live religious-looking lives but have hearts that are disobedient and far away from God are achieving nothing. God is no fool. He can see right through people's schemes and pretences. Outward displays of piety will not develop intimacy with God.

Fruits of Intimacy

The beauty of an intimate relationship with God is that it brings with it the fruit of obedience. When I experienced what I have described as a baptism of God's love, a doorway to intimacy with God was opened: I was caught up in a positive cycle of grace. As I got to know God through prayer and Bible reading and as I discovered how wonderful he was, my relationship with him grew deeper; and as my relationship with him grew deeper, I had a greater desire to obey him, because the relationship was so fulfilling that I did not want jeopardize it by being disobedient.

There is a place of fulfillment in God available to us that will bring the kind of satisfaction Paul talks about in Philippians. When we find that place, we will guard it with our very lives.

Yes most certainly, and I count all things to be loss for the excellency of the knowledge of Christ Jesus, my Lord, for whom I suffered the loss of all things, and count them nothing but refuse, that I may gain Christ and be found in him, not having a righteousness of my own, that which is of the law, but that which is through faith in Christ, the righteousness which is from God by faith; that I may know him, and the power of his resurrection, and the fellowship of his sufferings, becoming conformed to his death; if by any means I may attain to the resurrection from the dead. (Phil. 3:8–11)

Paul had reached such a deep level of intimacy with Christ that he considered everything else to be worthless. His desire was not only to know Christ and his resurrection power but also to enter into Christ's sufferings. This is real friendship. A true friend is one who will enter into joy and victory with you and will also enter into grief and suffering with you. We can experience this kind of relationship with God. In my Christian walk I have had the privilege of weeping with God over those who have not yet found him and rejoicing with him and his angels over one sinner who turned to God.

A Word of Caution

The value Jesus places on intimacy with him is apparent in the story of Mary and Martha in Luke 10:38–42. The passage indicates that God values our intimacy above our service.

It happened as they went on their way, he entered into a certain village, and a certain woman named Martha received him into her house. She had a sister called Mary, who also sat at Jesus' feet, and heard his word. But Martha was distracted with much serving, and she came up to him, and said, "Lord, don't you care that my sister left me to serve alone? Ask her therefore to help me." Jesus answered her, "Martha, Martha, you are anxious and troubled about many things, but one thing is needed. Mary has chosen the good part, which will not be taken away from her."

In this story Mary chooses to sit at Jesus' feet rather than serve Jesus. I don't believe that God is short of servants. There are many angels in heaven who serve God; some, for example, worship him day and night (Rev. 4:8) and some run errands, so to speak (Luke 1:19). It seems reasonable, therefore, that the greatest thing God wants from us is not our service but our intimacy. In the place of intimacy with him, God speaks to us things that we could never hear in the busyness of serving him.

God is not the great task master in the sky but rather our great Father walking alongside us. His desire is to develop an intimate friendship with us. Within that relationship we will hear his voice, feel his love, and experience his power. We must make sure that in the Christian life we do not settle for any cheap imitations void of genuine fellowship with God. Our reward and our goal is nothing less than God himself.

UP

DOWN

IN

OUT

Section B

Look DOWN into ourselves

DOWN

4. What Must I Do to Be Saved?

I stood in the shower recently and decided it was time to start drawing some conclusions on the question, what must I do to be saved? This is a question I had been wrestling with for a long time. You may wonder why this thought came to me in the shower. Well, the shower is one of the places where I meet with God. It is ideal because I can shout and sing and people can't hear much of what is going on. I have received many revelations in the shower.

But maybe a better question to start with is, what *did* I do to be saved?—because I would like to think that I am already saved. My answer could be: I stood up in a meeting after hearing a gospel message and repeated a prayer. In fact, I did this quite a few times. My mum says that I even stood up once after she gave a stirring message at a gospel service back home in Sierra Leone. She thinks I might have done it to be nice, because no one else stood up.

I have to confess that I have grown rather cynical of some of our methods of evangelism and ideas about "conversion."

Before I went to university, I did a year-long course in evangelism and biblical studies at a congregation in Yorkshire. I learned a lot during this time. The Bible teaching, training in evangelism, and preaching were excellent, and I got the chance to coauthor a booklet on cults and other religions. (I guess this isn't my first publication after all.) The highlight of the training was the opportunity to be mentored by a gifted evangelist.

Strangely, however, after my year of training I found myself at university feeling disillusioned and slowly drifting away from God. One of my major questions at the time was whether our methods of evangelism really work, and I had begun to believe the answer was a resounding no. My own methods did not seem to work well. Maybe my expectations were too high, or maybe I hadn't tried hard enough, though I don't think that was the case. I had memorized key scriptures. I had learned the equivalent of the four spiritual laws. I had gone to schools and preached the gospel. I had been overseas and preached there too. I had done all kinds of things, but I had not seen a whole lot of fruit.

It has taken me a long time to get to grips with these questions regarding salvation and evangelism, and I still do not have all the answers. But God has been kind enough to give me some insights into the gospel that we preach, the methods that we use in evangelism, and the "requirements" for becoming a Christian, or even better, a follower of Christ.

Methods of Evangelism

I am suspicious of things like the four spiritual laws and other mechanistic ways of so-called conversion. For example, I learned about the four Rs, which can be summarized as follows:

- Recognize that you are a sinner in need of Christ
- Repent of your sins
- Receive salvation through the forgiveness of sins bought on the Cross
- Respond by walking in obedience to Christ's commands, including things like baptism in water and receiving the Holy Spirit

Many of us would agree that a sermon that expanded and gave background on these four points would be a good gospel presentation. And if someone had heard and grasped the sermon or some other presentation of the four Rs, we might invite him or her to say a prayer, perhaps one on the back of a tract. The prayer would probably repeat some of the four Rs, but with an emphasis on repentance and asking Jesus into your heart as your personal Savior. This again is something we would consider normal and acceptable, and we would greatly rejoice as we declared that we had a new brother or sister born into the kingdom of God.

The thing is, although the Bible says that Jesus went around preaching the gospel, I never see him preaching anything remotely like the four Rs. The practice of saying a prayer to ask Jesus into your heart is also one that I do not find in the New Testament. I am not saying that people who have heard a 4Rs sermon and said a prayer on the back of a tract are not Christians, but I am not saying that they *are* Christians, either. I believe that becoming a Christian is something a little bit more substantial than that.

The gospel that Jesus preached wasn't like what many people preach today. For starters, Jesus preached about the kingdom, which is something the average Christian is still getting his head

UP

DOWN

IN

OUT

round. Jesus' message carried the theme: repent for the kingdom of God is close by (Matt. 4:17; Mark 1:14–15). It seems to me that this message of the kingdom (which wasn't a three-point sermon) was present in all of Jesus' ministry. Jesus did not just preach the gospel; he lived it and he was it. *He* was good news to people. He healed the sick, cleansed lepers, raised the dead, and declared that these acts were signs that the kingdom was in our midst.

I believe that the average salvation-only gospel message sells the kingdom short. Salvation gets us into the door of the kingdom, but there is a lot more beyond that. Jesus' death on the Cross was not an end in itself but a means to an end. Its purpose was to remove the effect and power of sin so that we might not only enter into a fresh encounter with God but also share in his holiness and experience his divine power that gives us everything we need for life and godliness. The good news is that, thanks to what Jesus has done on the cross, we have been set free and can enter the life that the Father intends for us, and that is to know him and be coheirs and coworkers with Christ.

Believe and You Will Be Saved

The biblical requirement for "being saved" is simply to believe—to believe in Christ and to believe in his gospel.

> They said, "Believe in the Lord Jesus Christ, and you will be saved, you and your household." (Acts 16:31)

> Jesus came into Galilee…saying, "The time is fulfilled, and the Kingdom of God is at hand! Repent, and believe in the Good News." (Mark 1:14–15)

He who believes and is baptized will be saved; but he who disbelieves will be condemned. (Mark 16:16)

On one level the call to believe may seem simple and easy. But in reality, although it may be simple, I'm not so sure about the easy part. For many people today, *belief* is an intellectual word and has more to do with mental assent than anything else. We live in a world where it is acceptable to have an abstract or theoretical belief in something without it having any major impact on our life. This was not the kind of belief that Jesus or Paul and Silas were referring to in the passages above. In the Jewish culture, to believe in something meant that you lived it out. For someone to say that he was a Jew who believed in Yahweh meant that his whole life revolved around Judaism. He would be a regular at the synagogue and the temple and would observe the laws and feasts of Jewish tradition. This is a huge contrast to our modern approach to belief, where we can say, "Yeah, I believe in God," and do little or nothing about it.

True belief in God has massive implications for an individual; it forces a person to ask questions such as, what is God like? what does he want from me? and, what do I want from him? These questions cannot be answered by doing nothing; they must be answered through active pursuit. True belief is substantial and will inevitably lead to action of some kind. Believing in Jesus naturally leads to things like being baptized and seeking to connect with God through prayer and reading the Bible. Although doing such things does not necessarily mean that we believe, believing should lead to outward expressions.

When we ask if someone is a Christian, we may have in mind whether the person has prayed a prayer of repentance or whether he or she believes the same things that we believe. Our focus is on a specific set of actions that makes someone part of the in-crowd or on intellectual ideas that we call faith or belief. I have been in situations where a person who has said the sinner's prayer, believes certain things, and turns up to church on Sundays is declared a Christian. It doesn't seem to matter what the person gets up to the rest of the week or how little change has occurred in his or her life.

In reality, we are called to be disciples more than we are called to carry the label "Christian." The word *Christian* is found only three times in the New Testament, but the word *disciple* is commonly used by the gospel writers to refer to a believer. Discipleship speaks of relationship, commitment, and ongoing learning. The view that Christianity is primarily about a one-time conversion experience is a galaxy away from Jesus' intentions. The conversion experience ("becoming a Christian" or "being born again") does not have to be our primary focus in our quest to fulfill the Great Commission (Matt. 28:18–20). Our focus should be on making disciples. And in my experience, becoming a Christian is the easy bit. Being a disciple is much harder.

What Is a Disciple?

The question we should be asking is not, what must I do to be saved? but, how can I become a disciple? A disciple is someone who is a learner or an apprentice of a teacher. It is someone who so strongly believes in the message of the teacher that he or she not only listens and learns from the teacher but also spreads the teaching to others. The concept of a disciple is not something we are used to in the Western world today. The idea that Jesus had followers who abandoned everything to follow him around and learn from him is alien to us.

Imagine that a man today quit his job in order to learn everything he could from a particular teacher. The man traveled with the teacher all over the place. He modeled himself on the teacher and even taught others the things he had learned from the teacher. We would think such a person was weird and maybe even irresponsible for giving up his job, especially if he had a family to support.

This, however, helps us understand what it means to be a disciple of Jesus. It is to be willing and able to abandon everything in a wholehearted pursuit of the Master and his teachings. Not only to watch him and listen to him, but also to do the things he did. Not only to believe in the things he taught, but also to practice them and to teach others to practice them.

A weakness in our Western culture is that learning has become focused more on receiving information and less on application. That is why people can call themselves Christians and believe all the right things but not apply the truth to their lives. It has always fascinated me that someone can be a theologian and not be a Christian or not even believe in God. This can only be possible when the practice of faith and knowledge about faith are separated into distinct functions. As Christians we are called not simply to be people who learn and believe certain doctrines but to be obedient disciples.

Being Disciples Today

What does being a disciple look like today? The biggest mark of a disciple of Jesus is a love of Jesus that leads to obedience. Today, just as it was in the first century, those who are called to follow Jesus should stand out in the way they obey Jesus and his commands. They should be passionately devoted to Christ in every way. They should be devoted to him, above all, as a person with whom they have a relationship. They should be devoted to his teaching, they should be devoted to his purposes, and they should also be devoted to his lifestyle.

In the Great Commission found in Matthew 28, Jesus states what our mission is:

> Jesus came to them and spoke to them, saying, "All authority has been given to me in heaven and on earth. Go, and make disciples of all nations, baptizing them in the name of the Father and of the Son and of the Holy Spirit, teaching them to observe all things that I commanded you. Behold, I am with you always, even to the end of the age." Amen. (Matt. 28:18–20)

Our job is to make disciples of all nations. And how do we do this? We are to teach them to obey all that Jesus has commanded us.

This commission was given directly to the first disciples and indirectly to us. If they were supposed to do and teach all that they were taught, then by deduction we are supposed to do all that *they* did and were taught, since we are the result of their obedience to the initial command. Anything less than teaching people to obey Jesus is not discipleship. No amount of information and sharing of knowledge can replace the simple fact that we are called to obey and teach others to obey.

Maybe our problem today is that we cannot teach others to do that which we ourselves have never been taught to do. Paul says what the purpose of his preaching was:

For I will not dare to speak of any things except those which Christ worked through me, for the obedience of the Gentiles, by word and deed, in the power of signs and wonders, in the power of God's Spirit; so that from Jerusalem, and around as far as to Illyricum, I have fully preached the Good News of Christ. (Rom. 15:18–19)

Paul's goal was the obedience of the Gentiles. Paul achieved this through the preaching of the gospel. If we preach the full gospel in the power of the Spirit using words, deeds, signs, and wonders, the end product will be unbelievers coming to faith in and obedience to Christ.

But we can be caught in a vicious cycle: when we don't fully preach the gospel, we end up with disciples who don't fully preach the gospel, and so on. We have to break the cycle at some point either by fully preaching the gospel or by becoming true disciples, otherwise we will never get anywhere.

Consumers of Religious Goods and Services

At a conference I attended, Christian author Dallas Willard posed a question we should all ask ourselves. To paraphrase, he asked, "Does the gospel I preach have a natural tendency to produce disciples or merely consumers of religious goods and services?"

There is no shortage of consumers in our churches today, but do we have disciples? If we go to some Christian communities, we are inundated with a whole host of goods such as books and tapes, and services such as conferences, dating groups, and weight-loss programs. I recently read in a newspaper about a

UP

DOWN

IN

OUT

Christian couple who set up a website to sell sex toys and other such things for Christians. It is easy to get sucked into the Christian consumer world. This world is not all that different from the secular consumer world except that it attaches words like *Christian, Jesus, church,* and *Bible* to the things it sells.

The difference for many people when they become Christians is that instead of just buying loads of CDs and books as they did before, they now specifically buy Christian CDs and books. I recently saw an ad for a Christian conference on a cruise ship. I have nothing against conferences or cruises, but I don't see why the two need to be put together. I fear that it could be an excuse for Christians to live lavish lifestyles by sticking the label "Christian" on it so people don't feel guilty about it. I have started to think that in calling so many things "Christian" that have little to do with Christ, we might actually be taking the name of the Lord in vain. At any rate, many of the "Christian" goods and services can blind us to the true state of our souls.

Robert Burnell wrote an amazing story titled *Escape from Christendom* (originally published by Bethany House, 1980). It is a God-given dream that serves as a wake-up call to the body of Christ. The story reveals a significant difference between "Christian City" and the "City of God." Christian City is full of religious goods and services. It is glamorous, it is attractive, and it is comfortable. It is much easier to get to this place than the City of God. Today many people have made their home in Christian City and do not even realize that there is a City of God beyond the horizon. Though it is harder to get to the City of God, the journey is worth it, because there we will find God himself. Not a cheap imitation or substitute. The real thing.

It is a travesty that we can take on the label "Christian" without any real inner transformation and outward change, that we can continue living as selfishly as before within a world of religious goods and services. I have a friend who became a Christian consumer but never really became a Christian. I must admit with great sadness that many of her friends, including me, did not realize this for nearly two years. Today my friend is neither a Christian consumer nor a Christian in any other sense.

Marks of New Testament Christianity

I believe that as Western Christians transition into true followers of Christ, certain marks of New Testament Christianity will become a reality to us.

Suffering

In many nations around the world, people who follow Christ face tremendous persecution from the authorities. I sometimes wonder what would happen to consumers of religious goods and services if they lived in times of persecution. It is easy to associate with Christians and label yourself a Christian when little or no cost is involved. But when, for example, you might be killed after you are baptized, as is the case in parts of India, it is much more difficult and costly to call yourself a Christian.

One of the marks of being a real follower of Christ is a willingness to suffer for Christ. Many of Jesus' original apostles experienced great suffering and died violent deaths for his name's sake. During the reign of Nero the followers of Christ were willing to be thrown to lions, beheaded, and used as human torches, all for the sake of Christ. When the church faces such persecution, consumers of Christian goods and services are practically nonexistent. During times of persecution a person must come to genuine faith in order to believe that Christ is worth dying for. I admit that brand-new Christians may take a little while to mature to the point where they are willing to suffer for Christ's sake; but this is a product of the cultural climate that we live in. In nations where persecution is common, it is the other way around: until a person truly believes, he or she does not call himself or herself Christian.

Signs and wonders

Another mark of New Testament Christianity is performing signs and wonders. Those who follow Christ are to do what Christ did, which included healing the sick, raising the dead, and all kinds of other miracles. Some people today believe that we are no longer supposed to be involved in supernatural ministry. It is quite astonishing that people who claim to believe that the commission of Mark 16:15–18 applies to all Christians would somehow not believe that healing the sick is among the things that Jesus commands his disciples to do and teach others to do. This is another demonstration of the fact that we are living our own Christianity that is a cheap imitation of the real thing. This is a man-made rather than a God-ordained faith. Such Christianity does not even need God. How hard can it be to read the Bible, talk about it, and go to church meetings? That does not require supernatural enablement. Healing the sick and raising the dead, however, will not happen without God's involvement.

Love and unity

A church that is full of disciples should also experience God's supernatural enablement for love and unity. One of Jesus' priorities in his prayer in John 17 was unity for his church—that they would be of one heart and one mind, as he is with the Father and the Holy Spirit. One of the greatest struggles of the church today is disunity. There are so many different denominations, all with their own emphases. Some denominations are so passionate about doctrinal interpretations that they are willing to reject Christian brothers and sisters who hold different beliefs but who nevertheless love the Lord just as much as they do, if not more. This is tragic considering that Jesus said his disciples would be known by their love for one another (John 13:35).

Those who follow Christ will be like him in his openness and acceptance. Jesus never said we would be known for the purity of our doctrine. For us to stop loving each other over doctrinal differences suggests to me that we think we know better than Christ. The priorities of a true disciple will be lined up with his teacher's. The fact that we can be so divided and act so unlovingly is a sign that we are living something that falls short of biblical faith.

I have never been able to understand people who make it their mission and ministry to pull down and destroy other people's ministries. They claim to love the body of Christ too much to allow heresy, but if they loved the body, they would also love the person whose ministry and life they were destroying for sport. I very much believe in holding people accountable for what they do and teach; however, the person with the primary responsibility of judging is Christ himself (Rom. 2:16; 2 Tim. 4:1). James says that teachers will be judged more harshly (James 3:1), and I assume that Christ will be the one doing the judging.

When we make holding correct doctrines our primary responsibility, we not only bring division to the body of Christ, but we also bring a lot of hurt and confusion. Jesus says love should be the mark of his disciples. Anyone who thinks otherwise will have to take that up with Jesus.

UP

DOWN

IN

OUT

Holiness

As disciples, our goal should be lives that reflect the Master in every way, including his character, holiness, and moral purity. The danger of a church obsessed with outward appearance is that many times people can attend church and perform many other religious rituals but in their hearts remain unchanged. If we took time to search our hearts instead of busying ourselves with activities, we might find much inside of us that does not reflect Christ. If we would only come to him, he would not only forgive our sins but also begin a process of transforming specific areas of our lives.

Sin need no longer be a problem for true disciples in the way that it is for those who have not encountered the saving power of Christ. To be holy, we must constantly experience the forgiveness of Christ and the transforming power of Christ. Both were let loose by the miracle of the Cross. More and more today, people are bringing the name of Christ into disrepute by lives that have never been brought under the cleansing and transforming power of Jesus' work on the Cross. We can be perfect and holy like Christ only if we walk with him daily, listen to him daily, and experience his love and power daily. This holiness should be the natural fruit of being a disciple.

Are We Disciples?

It amazes me how badly we can miss the point. My mum once taught me that we often have blind spots that we cannot see and need others to help us see. This has relevance not only on an individual, personal level but also on a corporate level. As the church we need to start listening to those outside the church who say that we are hypocritical and selfish. Although such remarks are not always true, there may be more truth in some statements than we would like to admit. These comments are not the persecution Jesus was talking about, as some would like to believe. These are comments made by people who see us as we truly are.

As the body of Christ we need to reexamine our call to follow Christ. Is it only about a conversion experience, or is it about a lifetime of following? Are we simply saved, or are we disciples? Can we even be simply saved? Do our lives reflect the one we call Master?

The question we must continue to ask ourselves is not, what must I do to be saved? but, what must I do to follow Christ?

UP

DOWN

IN

OUT

85

5. The god of All Comfort

Ask yourself this question: Do I worship the god of all comfort? Observant people will notice that *god* is spelled with a small *g*. There is a reason for this.

In 2 Corinthians 1:3 God is described as the God of all comfort: "Blessed be the God and Father of our Lord Jesus Christ, the Father of mercies and God of all comfort." The word translated as "comfort" comes from the same root as the word *Comforter* used to refer to the Holy Spirit. This Greek root, *parakaleo*, can mean consolation, encouragement, or teaching. I have heard the English word *comforter* used for a stick to poke sheep with when they begin to lag behind; this relates well with the meaning of *parakaleo* as teaching or instructing. *Parakaleo* can also convey the idea of coming alongside to help or encourage.

God is indeed the God of all comfort who desires to help us and encourage us along the way. Many of us need God's help, encouragement, and comfort. I have met people who have gone through horrible experiences, and it was only when the Comforter came to their side that they found healing and restoration. The next verse (2 Cor. 1:4) tells us that the purpose of God's comforting us is that we might comfort others—that "we may be able to comfort those who are in any affliction, through the comfort with which we ourselves are comforted by God."

Despite this biblical definition of comfort, Christians have seemingly turned another kind of comfort into a god. The Oxford English Dictionary defines comfort as "a state of physical ease and freedom from pain or constraint." This kind of comfort has its place, but it was never meant to be our sole goal in life. Yet for many who call themselves Christians today, this comfort *has* become the goal, at the expense of obedience to Christ. Let me share more about my early Christian days to describe what I am talking about.

Early Days

As mentioned before, one of the main things that characterized my initial Christian commitment was fear of hell and of the God who sent people to hell. This was a result of the preaching that I received in my birth country of Sierra Leone.

After moving to the UK, I heard another gospel preached from the pulpits—what some now call the prosperity gospel. This gospel was not in those days the kind of financial prosperity gospel that abounds in some corners of the church today; it was a milder and more general form but was equally as unhelpful as "God is a cash cow" messages. The message was simple: "Come to Jesus and everything will be all right." In our society, such a message is attractive, but it is particularly attractive if you come from a country that the United Nations has described as the least developed nation in the world. This everything-will-be-all-right message was what I was exposed to, and it motivated me as a Christian for several years.

UP

DOWN

IN

OUT

What impact did the prosperity gospel have on me? For one, it never prepared me for hardships. My attitude was: "I should no longer have any problems, and if I do, it means that God is not fulfilling his part of the deal, so why should I fulfill my part?" This attitude was a contributory factor to my unstable walk with God in my early days as a Christian. I did not expect suffering or difficulty. I did not even expect an increase in temptations. I did not realize that when I had changed sides, Satan had declared war on me. As a result, I went through difficult times in my faith.

Before I made a commitment to follow Christ, I wasn't such a bad kid. I didn't go out drinking and smoking like many of my peers did. I had few relationships with girls and was not the type to be sleeping around. But after I made a commitment to Christ I found myself struggling with all kinds of temptations that I had never struggled with before, and I gave in to some of them. This puzzled me, because I thought that this was not the way becoming a Christian was supposed to be.

Not only did the prosperity gospel leave me unprepared for the challenges and struggles I would face, it did not prepare me for the things that God would require of me. I had expected obeying and serving God to be easy, but it was not. My response to hardship turned out to be disobedience. Fortunately God began to open my eyes to the reality of what being a Christian is and the challenges that come with it. Obedience is not always easy, but it is always right.

My Call to Ministry

The revelation about the struggles of Christian life came during a period that I would describe as my first true calling to ministry.

I was at a week-long camp for young people from our network of churches. It was one of the best Bible weeks I have ever been to. Every night a Christian DJ played dance remixes of popular Matt Redman and Delirious songs and a whole host of other high-energy contemporary worship songs. These were some of the best worship times I have ever experienced in a churchlike setting.

Back to the point. During this week, God began drawing my attention to certain scriptures. The first one was the story of the apostle Paul's call to ministry, when God talks to Ananias about Paul. "But the Lord said to him, 'Go your way, for he is my chosen vessel to bear my name before the nations and kings, and the children of Israel. For I will show him how many things he must suffer for my name's sake'" (Acts 9:15–16). I am not deluded enough to think that my calling is equal to that of the apostle Paul, but I do believe that God was speaking to me personally through this scripture. I loved the first part of the scripture—the idea of being a chosen vessel—but I was not so keen on the second part—suffering for the Lord's sake. This didn't make sense to me. *If I am God's chosen instrument for ministry,* I thought, *then why do I have to suffer? In fact, what has suffering got to do with Christianity?*

I began to search the Bible and soon realized that it was laden with promises of suffering for those who love Jesus. For example, Philippians 1:29 says that "it has been granted to you on behalf of Christ, not only to believe in him, but also to suffer on his behalf." This almost makes suffering sound like a privilege, but suffering definitely did not sound like a privilege to me. I discovered many other scriptures that made it clear that suffering and persecution were a natural part of being a Christian (see John 15:20; Rom. 8:17; 2 Tim. 3:12).

As I looked deeper into the life of Paul, I was struck by the suffering he experienced.

> Are they servants of Christ? (I speak as one beside himself) I am more so; in labors more abundantly, in prisons more abundantly, in stripes above measure, in deaths often. Five times from the Jews I received forty stripes minus one. Three times I was beaten with rods. Once I was stoned. Three times I suffered shipwreck. I have been a night and a day in the deep. I have been in travels often, perils of rivers, perils of robbers, perils from my countrymen, perils from the Gentiles, perils in the city, perils in the wilderness, perils in the sea, perils among false brothers; in labor and travail, in watchings often, in hunger and thirst, in fastings often, and in cold and nakedness. Besides those things that are outside, there is that which presses on me daily, anxiety for all the assemblies. (2 Cor. 11:23–28)

What, we might ask, did Paul not suffer from?

Having gained an understanding of suffering as a part of the Christian life, I certainly did not enter into ministry expecting to become some kind of pop star or anything like that. In fact, I expected the kinds of things that Paul described to happen to me. So far, however, I have not experienced much of that, though I have had a few close encounters. Once when I was in Poland on a mission trip with my youth group, I was chased by three neo-Nazi Satanists who wanted to beat me up on two counts: for being black and being a Christian. During another outreach I had eggs thrown at me (but luckily none of them hit me). Even more bizarre was the time kids threw water balloons at our team. This I didn't actually object to so much because it was a very hot day and being hit could have proved quite refreshing.

24/7 Prayer Room

I find myself disturbed by the way many Christians are obsessed with being comfortable and abhor the idea of suffering. No wonder the excesses of prosperity teaching have found fertile ground to flourish in our midst.

A while ago our church organized a week of 24/7 prayer. Time in the prayer room has always been significant for me. The first time that I helped organize a week of prayer, I ended up with the promise of a wife which was fulfilled within a year (that's enough to motivate any young person to try 24/7 prayer). On this occasion I was in the prayer room crying out to God for my neighborhood and the young people in it. I was seeking ideas and strategies to reach them and was asking God why the Christians had not yet made much of an impact in the area. God answered my questions with some insight and revelation that I did not expect. I felt him say that one reason we had not made more headway was that, on the whole, we were unwilling to choose sacrifice and endure suffering. We tended to seek the path of least resistance.

I took my time to meditate on this word, and I saw how it applied not only to my life but to the lives of many people in our churches today. As we look through the history of the church, we see that it is those who were willing to choose sacrifice and endure suffering that we now look upon as heroes of the faith. Let's look at some of these figures.

Heroes of Faith

We can begin with Abraham, who had to leave the comforts of home to embark on a journey when he wasn't quite sure where he would end up. If we had a friend who decided to do that these days, we would probably tell the person that he or she was being irresponsible. Imagine our comments: "Think about your studies," "Did God really say that?" "How are you going to live?" But Abraham was willing to stick his neck out and make himself uncomfortable. He left his home to find another home where God dwelt.

Take John Wesley. One of the reasons he had such a remarkable ministry was that he traveled thousands of miles on horseback preaching the gospel. This is hardly a comfortable form of transport. He considered hardship and persecution such a natural thing that it is reputed that he was once alarmed by a lack of persecution. The story goes like this. One day Wesley was riding his horse on one of his trips when he realized that he had not been persecuted that day. So he got off his horse and knelt by a bush to pray and seek the Lord on the matter, asking if he had fallen out of favor with the Lord. While he was praying, a local chap with whom Wesley was not very popular saw him and threw a rock at him, just missing him. Wesley then got up, thanked the Lord that he was still in his favor, and got back on his horse to continue his journey.

William Booth did not start The Salvation Army—the most well-known Christian mercy ministry movement in the world—without making sacrifices. Although there are many places where Christians are not just unpopular but are actually unwelcome, The Salvation Army has such a positive reputation for its charitable deeds that it is welcome almost everywhere. Booth made many sacrifices to see this movement develop. He had to leave his family and go to London to pursue his call. He even got barred from preaching in Methodist congregations because he resigned his position to do evangelism. Working with the poorest of the poor is something that will definitely take you out of your comfort zone. William Booth successfully birthed a servant movement for the poor that still lives on today.

As a final example, I draw on the life of Rees Howells, who is well known for his amazing prayer life and the answers to his prayers. As a result of his answering God's call, not only did he have to leave behind the security of his job, but he had to leave behind his newborn son. You might not agree with this decision, but you have to admire Howells's willingness to sacrifice. Today he is known not only as a powerful intercessor and revivalist but for his involvement in the founding of a Bible college and children's homes. His life was full of faith and answered prayers.

A strong prayer life does not develop overnight but comes about through sacrifice. It comes through giving up comforts and setting aside time from our busy schedules to pray and seek God. This does not come effortlessly. If we would only accept this fact and realize that prayer requires a good measure of sacrifice, we would probably pray more. Instead, people expect that good Christians find prayer easy, and when they find it hard, they end up in a place of guilt and shame, thinking they are second-class Christians. This leads to even less prayer.

Life in the West

Many of us live in the Western world where freedom of speech, freedom of expression, and freedom of religion are strongly embraced values. We don't have to experience prison or beating for the sake of Christ on a regular basis.

Because of this, it is easy to spiritualize scriptures that talk about persecution and suffering. We might interpret Jesus' call to "take up your cross" (Matt. 16:24) as bearing a spiritual cross of prayer. Or we might see talk of persecution as spiritual attack from the devil in terms of worry or stress. Even if we don't spiritualize them, we end up thinking that persecution will be so far ahead in the future that it becomes irrelevant to us now. I don't expect us to manufacture the conditions that persecuted Christians face in many parts of the world, but I do expect us to take seriously Christ's call to deny ourselves daily, take up our cross, and follow him.

You may be thinking, *So what great sacrifices are* you *making then? What great suffering are* you *enduring?* The truth is, if I tell you what sacrifices I make, I am likely to fall into pride. But whatever sacrifices I am making, or suffering I am enduring, there is room for greater sacrifices. One of the most important lessons I have learned as a Christian is that I should not try to justify my falling short by reinterpreting or ignoring Scripture.

Several years ago jokes were going around about how the government kept redefining unemployment so that the statistics didn't look so bad to the public. Sometimes we redefine what is a sin and what is not. How many times have we heard phrases like "I didn't steal; I just borrowed"? Personally I have learned that it is better to agree with God in confession about my sins so I can receive the promise of cleansing (1 John 1:9) than redefine sin and remain bound by it.

I have to be honest with where I am in regard to sacrifice and be honest about my falling short.

Generosity in Every Way

The purpose of genuine sacrifice is not simply to appear virtuous but to advance the kingdom of God, especially by being a blessing to others. Isaiah 58 talks about the kind of fast that God desires of us.

> Isn't this the fast that I have chosen: to release the bonds of wickedness, to undo the bands of the yoke, and to let the oppressed go free, and that you break every yoke? Isn't it to distribute your bread to the hungry, and that you bring the poor who are cast out to your house? When you see the naked, that you cover him; and that you not hide yourself from your own flesh? Then your light shall break forth as the morning, and your healing shall spring forth speedily; and your righteousness shall go before you; the glory of Yahweh shall by your rear guard. Then you shall call, and Yahweh will answer; you shall cry, and he will say, "Here I am." If you take away from the midst of you the yoke, the putting forth of the finger, and speaking wickedly; and if you draw out your soul to the hungry, and satisfy the afflicted soul: then your light shall rise in darkness, and your obscurity be as the noonday; and Yahweh will guide you continually, and satisfy your soul in dry places, and make strong your bones; and you shall be like a watered garden, and like a spring of water, whose waters don't fail. Those who shall be of you shall build the old waste places; you shall raise up the foundations of many generations; and you shall be called The repairer of the breach, The restorer of paths to dwell in. (Isa. 58:6–12)

God encourages us not only to sacrifice food in seeking him but also to look to the needs of others. We will always find people in need around us: the hungry, the oppressed, the naked. If we see such needs and meet them, we are promised that God will hear the cries of our hearts; we will be guided by God, and our souls will be satisfied. But as far as God is concerned, for him to hear our prayers and respond to our cries, we must respond to the cries of the needy.

These verses provide a significant challenge for us with regard to the needy.

Fasting and other forms of sacrifice must come from the right motivation. If our fasting is rooted in love for God and others, then it will bear fruit.

In 1 Corinthians 13 Paul states that without love, giving our bodies to be burned is pointless. Love is about selflessness without selfish motives. Therefore, self-sacrifice that does not benefit others is not true sacrifice, because underneath it is some form of selfishness. For example, some religions encourage people to harm themselves or go on pilgrimages to receive a benefit, such as a higher status within the religion. These actions are not truly sacrificial; they are simply paying a price to get something in return. Once I watched a documentary on a Hindu priest who rolled hundreds of miles to a certain temple as a religious pilgrimage. According to 1 Corinthians 13, such acts of seemingly great sacrifice are pointless unless the motive is selfless love that benefits others.

Real sacrifice is accompanied by generosity, and boy do we need generosity these days. We live in a time when people hold onto whatever they have. We are highly possessive of our time, money, and talents. We can be so self-obsessed that we often do not even realize the needs of the world around us. But when we look at the life of Jesus, we see a man who was generous. He was generous with his time, he was generous with his powers, and he was generous, ultimately, with his life. "Greater love has no one than this, that someone lay down his life for his friends" (John 15:13). This verse, with its high standard of sacrifice and generosity, continues to haunt me. Couple this with another verse—"Jesus therefore said to them again, 'Peace be to you. As the Father has sent me, even so I send you'" (John 20:21)—and it's enough to freak anyone out. Jesus sends us out to live as sacrificially and generously as he lived.

UP

The Cost of Running Our Churches

DOWN

It seems that instead of obeying Christ's command to his disciples to go out in the same way that Christ went out, we are busy making up our own commands. Having heard some alarming reports, I am shocked by the amount of money churches spend on themselves. I heard of a church in the US that spent a million dollars on its sound system and another US church that spent the same on a chandelier. These stories, if they are true, really scare me. They show how much the church has missed the point of its existence. I saw the following report in an article titled "Key Trends in Christian Stewardship and Philanthropy" on the Generous Giving website (www.generousgiving.org):

IN

In 2000, nearly 97 percent of the entire income of all Christian organizations was spent on, and primarily benefited, other Christians at home or abroad: $261 billion spent on ministering to Christians, $7.8 billion on already-evangelized non-Christians, and $0.81 billion on unevangelized non-Christians. (From David B. Barrett and Todd M. Johnson, *World Christian Trends AD 30–AD 2000: Interpreting the Annual Christian Megacensus* [William Carey Library, 2001]).

OUT

In my opinion, the church of Jesus Christ is not following the example of the Master. Christ once said, "The foxes have holes, and the birds of the sky have nests, but the Son of Man has nowhere to lay his head" (Matt. 8:20). Somehow I don't think that Christ has the same concern for palatial surroundings as some people would like to claim.

Someone might respond, "Oh, we need to make God's house wonderful and beautiful," and quote Scriptures like Haggai 1:7–9:

> This is what Yahweh of Armies says: "Consider your ways. Go up to the mountain, bring wood, and build the house. I will take pleasure in it, and I will be glorified," says Yahweh. "You looked for much, and, behold, it came to little; and when you brought it home, I blew it away. Why?" says Yahweh of Armies, "Because of my house that lies waste, while each of you is busy with his own house."

But tell me, friends, does God dwell in houses made with hands? Paul is quite clear that the body is the temple of God (1 Cor. 6:19). God is calling us to sacrifice our plush surroundings in our wonderful modern cathedrals in order to build a spiritual house for Christ—made from living stones of believers from every nation, tribe, and tongue (1 Pet. 2:5; Rev. 5:9).

Sacrifice of Community

Embracing a call to sacrifice will greatly affect how we exist as a community of believers. Although it's easy to talk about community, in reality being a community is costly. The idea of iron sharpening iron suggests that in rubbing up against one another in community, each of us will lose some of who we are to be sharpened.

There are two essential components for successfully being in a community, and both involve self-sacrifice. The first is a willingness to give up your rights to your own way. As humans we have an innate desire to do as we please. Our inner battle cry is "My way or the highway." This desire is often what brings about the breakdown of a community. We must be willing to lay down personal preferences, or as the Bible says, we must "prefer one another" (Rom. 12:10). I have been part of groups where issues that caused division were not even biblical essentials but were simply people's preferences. Sometimes such preferences are hidden behind spiritual jargon, but at the end of the day there is, for example, no biblical command as to whether worship should be led with a guitar or a piano. Our willingness to lay aside personal preferences will directly determine how united a community can be. This is no easy task. It requires sacrifice.

The second component is a willingness to invest in the lives of others at personal expense. The Bible describes Christians as living stones being put together by God (1 Pet. 2:5). Each stone in a building supports the others, and for every stone that you take away, the building is weakened. In the same way we need to support one another in community. This support is costly because it will sometimes mean missing out on the things we enjoy having or doing in order to be a blessing to someone else. One Bible passage that has fascinated me for a long time is the story in Acts 2 of how people sold their land to provide for others. It is easy to read that on the pages of the Bible but much more difficult to do in reality. These gifts were given at great personal cost. How would you like to sell your house or car and give the money to a less fortunate person in your community?

If we truly want to build Christian communities, we must be willing to make these kinds of personal sacrifices.

Sacrifice of Compassion and Helping Others

Compassion is an interesting word. The Oxford English Dictionary defines it as "sympathetic pity and concern for the sufferings or misfortunes of others." Without action, however, compassion does not do the recipient of it much good. In my Christian life I have found that the choice to be compassionate, if I am going to be of any help to the needy, always ends in some kind of personal sacrifice.

One of the responsibilities of the church of Jesus Christ is to show compassion and mercy to our neighbors (see Luke 10:29–37), which, as I have said, always costs us something. It may cost us emotionally as we weep with those who weep. It may cost us financially as we give to the poor. It may cost us time as we spend time with the lonely. "He has shown you, O man, what is good. What does Yahweh require of you, but to act justly, to love mercy, and to walk humbly with your God?" (Mic. 6:8).

Christ, in his earthly ministry, always took pity on people, and it cost him his reputation and ultimately his life. We cannot expect to show mercy without being willing to sacrifice. Issues in our world today include child soldiers, child sex slaves, sweatshops, starvation, and hunger, to name just a few. It is my wholehearted belief that Jesus wants his body to be the answer to these problems, and these problems are impossible to address without a measure of personal sacrifice.

Sacrifice of Missions

If the church embraces sacrifice, more Christians will enter the mission field. People sometimes have glamorous views of mission work. I remember how all my illusions about missions were dispelled on a short-term mission trip to Uganda.

Before this trip, I had always fancied myself as a missionary and had a desire to go out to some far-flung place to serve the Lord. It would be exciting and fun, I thought, to experience new cultures. I never considered for a moment that it would be difficult. Although I had been on some overseas outreaches, these trips were easy in comparison to this next one.

In Uganda, all my glamorous missionary ideas were wiped away. I found myself in a village in the middle of nowhere with only one other missionary companion. I was eaten by mosquitoes. I suffered from diarrhea. I was surprised most by how lonely I felt even though I was among people. The cultural and language differences created a feeling of loneliness that I had never experienced before. I came away feeling unsure of whether I could do this for an extended time.

To be a missionary you must be willing to sacrifice a great deal. Many missionaries leave behind comfortable homes, fulfilling jobs, friends, and families. This is the reality of mission work. If we do not embrace a life of sacrifice, there is no way we are going to reach this world with the gospel of Jesus Christ.

Sacrifice of Reputation

Philippians 2:7 says that Jesus made himself of no reputation and took the form of a servant. If we want to become like Christ, our obsession with popularity has to go. There will always be a sector, or multiple sectors, of society with whom we are not popular. Christ was unpopular with the Pharisees for endangering their religious reputation, authority, and livelihood. Not only did he publically rebuke them, but he attacked their money-making schemes (Matt. 23; John 2:14–16). He was unpopular with the Jews for speaking the truth about how they treated truth-speaking prophets like him (Luke 4:24–29). He was unpopular with the Romans for calling himself a king and being a possible source of social unrest (John 19:12–13).

If Christ was so unpopular, then who are we to expect popularity in this world? Christ promises that we will face unpopularity in addition to receiving positive responses to our message. "Remember the word that I said to you: 'A servant is not greater than his lord.' If they persecuted me, they will also persecute you. If they kept my word, they will keep yours also" (John 15:20).

It seems that people care more about how others perceive them than how God perceives them. We all want to be respected and admired by those around us—especially in ministry—but we have to give up our rights to good reputations. As someone who preaches, I am often tempted to deliver the kind of sermon that tickles people's ears and makes them think that I am wonderful. Doing this would guarantee not only that I get another invite but that other churches or organizations will want me to come preach. On the other hand, if I follow in my Master's footsteps, there will be a mixture of responses to my preaching. Some people will receive the message, and others will reject the message and messenger.

From Sacrifice to Passion

The good news is this: we can get to a place where sacrifices seem less of a loss and more of a joy. We, like Christ, can endure much for the joy set before us. "Looking to Jesus, the author and perfecter of faith, who for the joy that was set before him endured the cross, despising its shame, and has sat down at the right hand of the throne of God" (Heb. 12:2).

A friend of mine once pointed out some of the extraordinary feats that people will do for love and not consider costly. She said this because I had stayed up all night talking to a girl and still got up in the morning and got on with my day. The sleep I lost was a sacrifice well worth making for the sense of exhilaration I then felt. As we grow in our relationship with God, his passions become our passions and his joys become our joys. Those duties that once seemed burdensome may even become a joy. Seeing that Christ did not consider his life too big a sacrifice for his beloved, what sacrifice could we make that is too great for our God?

David Livingstone once said, "If a commission by an earthly king is considered an honor, how can a commission by a Heavenly King be considered a sacrifice?" Serving Christ and being part of the building of his kingdom is indeed an honor. A well-known saying is "God is no man's debtor." There is no sacrifice that we might make for God that he will not reward in full both in this life or the next.

Many people believe that the church is entering a new season of life in which we will be in a position to fulfill the Great Commission. We have at our disposal the people, the technology, and most important, we still have the power of God. But all these resources, including the power of God, will be of no use if the people of God do not make the choices that are necessary to bring about the expansion of the kingdom through the preaching of the gospel, leading to the close of this age (Matt. 24:14). As we hasten the day of his return (2 Pet. 3:12), one of

UP

DOWN

IN

OUT

the greatest choices we face is whether to be comfortable or whether to make sacrifices.

What sacrifices do you need to make to obey the call of God on your life? What are you willing to lay down to reach the world? Over and over, on every step of the journey, we will find ourselves having to make these choices. With God's help we can make the right ones.

UP

DOWN

IN

OUT

6. Nurturing Christ in You

sometimes describe myself as a postmodern monk. For a long time a side of me has been drawn toward monasticism. When I read books written by mystics, monks, and contemplators, I think to myself what a life it would be to devote so much time to hearing and experiencing God. I dream of being in the desert somewhere, living a life of contemplation and prayer. To be really honest, I would like to go back in time. Unfortunately, neither God nor science has yet provided me with the means of time travel, so I will just have to make do with this postmodern world in which I find myself.

You may ask what appeals to me about a monastic life, and the answer is this: I have a simple desire to spend time in the presence of God, where the life of Christ can flow into my spirit. I used to think that I needed to be a Celtic monk from several hundred years ago to do this. Thankfully I have learned otherwise. I have learned that Christian growth and discipleship can take place anywhere, under any conditions. Whether we are the persecuted Christians of China or the free Christians of the USA, one of the illiterate Christians of Sierra Leone or a Cambridge scholar of England, we all have one thing in common: we can experience Christian growth and discipleship.

In my pursuit of Christlikeness I have often asked myself questions such as, what is discipleship? and, how can I grow as a Christian? For a long time I expected all my Christian growth to come from church attendance, especially from the good sermons I have been blessed with over the years. I have since discovered that although church attendance has contributed to my growth, it is just one of many vehicles that God uses to help me grow. At a conference several years ago, I was challenged by Jack Deere. He pointed out that Christians have some funny ideas about quiet times. They think that if they bore themselves silly by spending time alone reading the Bible and throwing out prayers in a religious manner, they will grow as Christians. There is a lot to be said for a disciplined life, but Deere's point was that it takes more than just reading the Bible and praying mechanically to grow as a Christian. If our goal is Christlikeness, then we need to allow the life of Christ to flow into us.

The apostle Paul said he labored so that Christ would be formed in the people he ministered to (Gal. 4:19). For Christ to be formed in *us*, we need an inflow of Christ from a variety of sources. This, I believe, is the key to discipleship. We must seek out and find the sources and avenues through which the life of Christ can flow into us. To use the example from above, if we think that the only way the life of Christ can flow into us is through Bible reading, we are greatly mistaken. We seem to forget that the early church did not have the benefit of the New Testament for their discipleship programs. God must have had other ways of speaking to the early Christians and nurturing their faith. For example, Paul encourages them to speak to one another with psalms and hymns and spiritual songs (Col. 3:16) and also to bring prophetic words to one another (1 Cor. 14:5).

Defining the Goal

It is important at this stage to explain how I view the purpose and process of discipleship. As mentioned in a previous chapter, I believe a major goal of discipleship is teaching Christians to obey Christ. Our greatest example of obedience is Jesus himself, who learned obedience through the things he suffered (Heb. 5:8). In the past I have made the mistake of thinking that the goal of discipleship is to acquire as much information as possible. I ignored the fact that, according to James, information without transformation leads to self-deception. "But be doers of the word, and not only hearers, deluding your own selves" (James 1:22). In fact, our ultimate goal is much more than obedience; it is to be like Christ. And as we become more like Christ by following him and daily receiving life from him, we can be transformed into his image and likeness.

Being a disciple is the process of becoming like one's master in every way possible. This is true in the Christian life in the following specific ways:

- We can have the mind of Christ. "'For who has known the mind of the Lord, that he should instruct him?' But we have Christ's mind" (1 Cor. 2:16).
- We have access to the same power that Christ had to perform miracles. "But if the Spirit of him who raised up Jesus from the dead dwells in you, he who raised up Christ Jesus from the dead will also give life to your mortal bodies through his Spirit who dwells in you" (Rom. 8:11). "Most certainly I tell you, he who believes in me, the works that I do, he will do also; and he will do greater works than these, because I am going to my Father" (John 14:12).

- We can experience the same depth of relationship that Christ did with his Father when he walked on the earth. "I in them, and you in me, that they may be perfected into one; that the world may know that you sent me, and loved them, even as you loved me" (John 17:23).
- We can walk in the same holiness and purity that Christ displayed. "But just as he who called you is holy, you yourselves also be holy in all of your behavior" (1 Pet. 1:15).

The list goes on and on. In short, I have come to believe that discipleship is the process of becoming conformed to the image of Christ. "For whom he foreknew, he also predestined to be conformed to the image of his Son, that he might be the firstborn among many brothers" (Rom. 8:29).

Postmodern Disciplines

As I have broadened my view of discipleship, I have been amazed at the ways in which we can be discipled. Any place, person, or event that shapes us into Christ's image is very much a part of the discipleship process. I would like to share with you some of the areas I have found the life of Christ flowing in my journey and how they have helped me become more like Christ.

Devotions

On a few occasions I have come across young people complaining about their struggle with quiet times. I have found that the problem is not so much that they lack discipline or passion for the Lord but that they have formulated an image in their minds of what a quiet time should look like. Then, when they struggle

to achieve this image, they assume that they have major problems and end up feeling condemned. Usually their idea of a quiet
time is based on something they have learned from a leader, a
loved one, or a popular book.

I personally have wrestled with condemnation in the area of
my devotional life for three main reasons:

- Trying to be like someone other than the person Jesus
  has called me to be
- Having problems with my method of devotion
- Not taking into account my own nature and personality

Let me discuss each of these in more detail. Firstly, I once
found myself in the trap of the devil's condemnation after reading about the life of John "Praying" Hyde, who had an excep-
tional prayer life that should serve as an inspiration to us all
but is definitely not supposed to be a source of condemnation.
John Hyde prayed for hours and hours each day, and I thought
I was supposed to do the same. It took me a while to come to
the place where God spoke to me and pointed out that many
other great men and women of God did not pray like John Hyde
either. What matters is that each of us fulfills God's personal call
on our lives. No doubt we are all called to pray, and pray much,
but what that looks like will be different for each of us.

Secondly, I have been caught in the trap of using very boring and ineffective devotional methods. For example, it took me
a while to discover that I was not getting much out of my Bible
reading because I was more interested in the volume of material
that I covered than in the material that I actually assimilated. I
sometimes found I had read several chapters and not only could
I not remember large portions of them but I also did not draw

any life-giving conclusions from the material. Many people will find that if they take the time to learn how to get the most out of devotional times, those times will not be as boring and fruitless as they seemed in the past.

Thirdly, I have sometimes failed to remember that every individual is created differently. People enjoy different things and learn in a variety of ways. People even have different ways to express love to another person. It seems insane to me that we sometimes teach people to worship, read the Bible, and pray a certain way and expect it to work for everyone. I share John Drane's frustration with the one-size-fits-all approach that we have adopted in the church. The title of his book, *The McDonaldization of the Church,* says it all.

Two obviously different types of people are outward, verbal-processing extroverts and inward, thought-processing introverts. I have noticed that many authors are introverts, so their teaching on devotional life is biased toward the introvert. That is why we have the idea of a "quiet time" with God in the first place—it must have been invented by an introvert. But some people don't want quiet times with God; they want noisy times with God when they can read the Scriptures out loud, talk to God out loud, and tell him what is going on in their hearts. The truth is, I am an introvert; therefore I am biased toward spending time in silence with God. But because I also recognize that my devotional life should not be completely limited by personality, I have also been known to get my guitar out and go wild in God's presence.

Prayer and Confession

Prayer for me has been a constant battle, and I have never become the "Praying" Hyde that I once hoped I would become.

In the process, however, I have learned a lot of useful principles. For a start, I now realize that prayer is not what I used to think it was. I used to think that prayer was bringing to God a list of requests for other people and asking him over and over again to help. I also assumed that good prayer was always done out loud. Having been to many prayer meetings in my home country of Sierra Leone, I assumed that the louder and longer a prayer was, the more likely God was to hear it and answer.

God has broadened my idea of prayer in the past few years—so much so that for me prayer is simply communication with God. One of the most exciting times for me was when I first learned to hold a conversation with God as I went about my daily business—simply chatting away like a madman throughout the day. This really cultivated an intimacy with God that I am still reaping the benefits of today.

I have to admit that I am one of those people who thrive on spontaneity. The idea of following one mode of prayer, or Bible study, is more like punishment than a blessing. So my prayer life looks different each day. Some days I present requests to God, other days I talk to him as my Father and friend, and sometimes I just listen and try to hear what is on his heart at the time. I am definitely not good at following fixed prayers or liturgies. The closest I ever come to that is praying the prayers in Scripture, but I hardly ever use prayers such as Patrick's Breastplate. I do enjoy the Celtic prayers in a group, but not really on my own.

Another aspect of prayer that has become significant for me is confession. Once when I was teaching some young people, we had an unexpected evening. It started with just hanging out and chatting but ended up with people's confession of things going on in their lives that were impacting how they felt about themselves and their relationship with God. This was one of those times that no one could have planned for or engineered—God was working in people's hearts. As people confessed, we took time to pray for them and made sure they knew they were loved and accepted and definitely not judged. The air was thick with the presence of God, and the Holy Spirit reminded me of a verse in James. "Confess your offenses to one another, and pray one for another, that you may be healed. The insistent prayer of a righteous person is powerfully effective" (James 5:16). This scripture was being lived out right before my eyes. Right then and there I could see people's lives being impacted. This inspired me to embrace confession to others and to the Lord.

Many Christians think that the only time they need to confess or repent is when they first say the sinner's prayer and make a commitment to follow Christ. The reality is that what Christ has done on the cross is a once-and-for-all event, but we need to continue to make its power real in our lives on a daily basis. Our righteousness comes from Christ, and the only way to achieve righteousness is through confession and repentance. As we receive this righteousness, the effectiveness of our prayers increases. Whether we make prayers of petition or have conversational prayers of intimacy with the Lord, our righteousness will influence their effectiveness.

Study of the Word

Reading and meditating on the Bible is something that comes much more easily to me than prayer. I find the Bible so fascinating that I not only enjoy reading it but also enjoy reading about it and thinking about biblical ideas and concepts. It might shock you to know that many days I do not read the Bible. At this point, some of you may want to put this book down and conclude that this author is not worthy of your time or attention. Don't rush to do that. Give me just a few more minutes to explain where I am coming from.

Because I do not open a Bible and read it on certain days does not mean that I'm not engaging with the Word of the Lord on those days. Joshua 1:8 makes a thought-provoking and challenging statement:

> This book of the law shall not depart out of your mouth, but you shall meditate on it day and night, that you may observe to do according to all that is written therein: for then you shall make your way prosperous, and then you shall have good success.

We are asked to meditate on the Word of the Lord day and night and not let it depart from our mouths, but not to spend a specific amount of time reading the Bible. Have you ever thought about how the early church coped without a New Testament or how persecuted Christians in the world today survive without access to the Bible? Are these people any less Christian than we are?

Many days when I do not read the Bible, I meditate on something that I have read previously or engage in conversation over the Scriptures. Other days I read books that help me understand the Bible and the concepts that it conveys. For me the key is not how much I read the Bible but how much I receive and respond to the Word of the Lord.

As a student at St. Andrews I was amazed by theology students and lecturers who knew the Bible pretty well but neither applied its truth nor even believed in God. The point of Bible study and meditation is to engage with the Word of the Lord, which leads to deeper intimacy with God and greater obedience. Anything that facilitates loving and obeying God is valuable.

Some people find devotionals or things such as one-year Bibles helpful. I too have found these useful, but only for specific seasons. My personality loves spontaneity and finds Bible-reading programs too restrictive. I like to explore whatever themes God is putting on my heart at any given moment in time. On the other hand, I recognize that some people love structured reading programs and that is how they can receive the Word of the Lord and develop greater intimacy with God. More power to them. As for me and my brain, we will enjoy spontaneity.

Worship

I remember a season in my Christian walk when I loved to worship God through songs of love and adoration. I would happily spend hours in a day writing and singing songs to God. I would put on worship CDs and sing my way through the whole CD just enjoying God and worshiping him.

I was recently listening to some teaching by Jack Deere from CLAN Gathering 2005. CLAN Gathering is the largest Christian conference in Scotland and often draws speakers from all over the world. Deere told the story of a young boy going blind who found great comfort and relief in opera music. Then Deere played a piece of music called "Nessun Dorma" sung by Andrea Bocelli, the young boy now grown up. The song was wonderful, and I was stirred afresh with passion for worship. I am no fan of opera, but good music moves me. I don't believe I am alone. Music moves many of us.

Depending on the kind of person you are, music can be a significant way of worshiping God, but it is obviously not the only way in which to worship God. I have a friend who worships God by taking a walk in nature and admiring God's workmanship and giving him the glory. He can happily spend hours walking around a nice garden or park enjoying God's handiwork.

One of my own favorite ways to worship God is through the reading of the Scriptures. I believe God is honored when we give the Bible a significant place in our lives. It shows we value his words to us. I was part of a cell group where we sometimes worshiped through writing poetry. Other times we wrote psalms that communicated our love and passion for God. I have also been in meetings where someone paints a picture during the worship time. This is a natural way for some people to worship God with their talents and abilities.

Beyond even our personal preferences is the fact that worship does not necessarily mean singing, walking, or whatever else we might do. Worship is something that comes from our heart. It is a bowing down of our inner being before God to honor him for who he is.

Psalm 22:3 says, "But you are holy, you who inhabit the praises of Israel." There is something powerful in knowing that as we praise and worship God, he takes his place among the praises. In my experience, I find that as I worship God, he draws closer; and as he draws closer, I have a genuine sense of his presence and increased intimacy. What better way is there to become more Christlike than to spend time in Christ's presence through worship?

Worshiping God is so powerful that it needs to be a regular part of our walk with him. It needs to occur not only on the corporate level, when we gather with other believers, but also in our personal lives, when we are alone.

Meditation

Joshua 1:8 encourages us to "meditate on [the word] day and night," and yet when many Christians hear the word *meditation,* they think of dodgy Eastern or New Age practices and run a mile away from it. Thankfully some Christians out there are helping us regain the art of meditation that the Bible invites us to practice. The big difference between Christian Scripture meditation and other forms of religious meditation is that instead of emptying ourselves we are trying to fill ourselves with the Word of Christ, that we might be transformed by it.

Meditation is when we take time to focus and reflect on biblical truth. One of my favorite words associated with meditation is *rumination.* This means to think deeply or ponder over a thought. *Rumination* can also describe what cows do when they chew the cud. A cow chews its food over and over again to get all the nutrition it can out of it. To draw the parallel, we can chew on truth in our minds over and over again to get all the goodness we can out of it. This is part of what it means to meditate.

I have to confess that being an introverted thinker I do love meditation and don't find it as hard as some of my extroverted talker friends. Thinking about a story or scripture over and over again in my mind comes naturally to me. Even if I am not trying to do this, I do it subconsciously. However, there is a place for us all to think intentionally through a scripture or a story and allow it to fill our minds with truth. I find that in the process of meditation amazing revelation comes from God that I would have missed had I not taken the time. These are the kind of insights that I know are from God because they are beyond my usual frame of thought.

An important final point to make is that meditation does not stop in our minds. Meditation has been powerful for me because it always leads to practical applications of truth. Whether or not I choose to apply the truth is up to me, but I cannot spend time meditating on God's truth without experiencing its power to change and transform me. In my experience, the discipleship process is greatly facilitated by meditation, and I challenge you to try it.

Books and media

A significant amount of material on Christian growth is available to us in the form of books, tapes, CDs, videos, MP3 files, e-books, and more. The fact that we have all of these resources readily available to us—whether through the Internet or by going to a local store or library—is probably as significant to us as the printing press was to fifteenth-century Christians. It absolutely amazes me that I have access to preachers and teachers from around the world—people whom I would not have the opportunity to receive input from otherwise. As I gain access to wisdom from all over the world, I am increasingly aware of and experiencing the concept of the global church. Obviously there is no substitute for being pastored or taught by someone personally, but recorded media and books are helpful supplements.

Media is even able to transcend time. I get a lot out of the writings of early Christian mystics. Such teaching would have been totally unavailable to me if it were not for the books they left behind. There have been times in my Christian walk when I have faced tough questions that no one around me could really answer, but I was able to find help from a book. I can honestly say that books have been invaluable in my Christian walk. In fact, I believe in books so much that I decided to write one.

As Christians living in an increasingly interconnected world, we have the privilege of accessing huge amounts of information that can teach us about God and help us draw closer to him. We must make the most of it.

Mentors

By far, one of the greatest ways of growth for me has been having personal mentors along the path of life. Looking at the example of Jesus, we see that being a mentor is no easy thing; it requires love and commitment. Jesus seemed to spend a lot of time with his disciples, talking with them and teaching them. There are not many times when we read an account about Jesus when his disciples are not present. Can you imagine spending most of your time with the people you are trying to disciple? There are times when Jesus even seemed to be trying to escape for some alone time, but they would pursue him and he would not turn them away (Mark 1:35–38; Matt. 14:13–14). Even when they messed things up or lacked faith, he did not give up on them. For example, Peter denied Jesus but Jesus still loved him and restored him (Matt. 26:75; John 21:15–19). We all need such mentors in our lives because they will seriously help shape and bring out the character of Christ in us.

In my view, to mentor someone is not only about support-ing the person and being an example to him or her but also about creating an environment in which he or she can grow. Paul, Silvanus, and Timothy did this among the Thessalonian Christians.

> But we were gentle among you, like a nursing mother cher-ishes her own children. Even so, affectionately longing for you, we were well pleased to impart to you, not the Good News of God only, but also our own souls, because you had become very dear to us. (1 Thess. 2:7)

118

Apart from my parents, I have had two mentors who have shared their lives with me and have significantly impacted me. The first was my mother in the faith, Libby, whom I met shortly after moving to the UK. She brought me to a place where I could connect with God and find faith for myself. She welcomed me into her home and treated me like one of her own. She encouraged me to grow in my faith and see the call of God on my life. I would even go so far as to say that if it were not for her, I might well be a drug dealer in Manchester in and out of prison, or maybe worse.

My second significant mentor was my pastor Ted at university, who gave me the freedom to discover who I was and the gifts that God had given me. He was willing to let me loose on his congregation even though I was pretty rough around the edges. He was an incredible example to me in many ways. I learned from how he preached, how he prayed, and how he treated people. He is the most fatherly leader I have ever seen. Not only did he make his pulpit available to me, but he took risks with me by entrusting me with some responsibilities in our church. He invited me to into his home and family. I remember one time when he drove me several hours across the country when he really did not need to. It was his way of showing me love. There was not a thing within his power that he would not have done for me. He showed me so much love and treated me like a son.

One thing these two mentors had in common was that they believed in me when there was not much to believe in, and they loved me when there was not much to love. They taught me many things I needed to know about God. I could talk to them openly and honestly about what was going on in my life without fear of condemnation. They were spiritual parents to me. Paul

UP

DOWN

IN

OUT

highlights the fact that we can have many tutors but not many spiritual parents. "For though you have ten thousand tutors in Christ, yet not many fathers. For in Christ Jesus, I became your father through the Good News" (1 Cor. 4:15). A parent is willing to give much more to his or her child than a tutor ever would be. Having mentors like this can make a massive difference in our Christian walk.

Friendships

Peer relationships are also significant in the discipleship process. As mentors can be to us like parents, peers will often challenge us in the same way that siblings do. In peer relationships, there will be times of encouragement and also times of tears. The advantage that peers often have over mentors is that they are in the same circles as us and can therefore see things in us that mentors might not be able to notice. "Iron sharpens iron; so a man sharpens his friend's countenance" (Prov. 27:17).

At university I had some friendships that fulfilled this proverb. I was part of a prayer and accountability group that met every other week. We were very open with and vulnerable to each other. We challenged each other in areas of weakness and also encouraged each other as we wrestled with the challenges of life. Much of my restoration to faith after a low period I owe to this group. There is a shaping that occurs as we rub up against one another—and even annoy each other—that can bring out the character of Jesus in us and enable us to experience the life of Christ flowing from one to another.

Another peer relationship that has kept me on track is my marriage. My wife is an incredibly loving and patient woman. One of the first things she brought into my life was healing through the tremendous acceptance she showed me. Our intimate relationship is not only a source of encouragement and accountability but also a means by which God can minister wholeness and inner healing through her unconditional love and acceptance. I have concluded that the source of much dysfunction in our lives is a lack of love and acceptance, and to have someone who will love us unconditionally can bring immeasurable restoration that leads to increased Christlikeness in our lives.

Whether with a marriage partner or a close buddy, peer relationships can have a significant impact on us. As we love one another, the life of Christ flows to us and through us.

Conferences and church meetings

There is a power that can flow in a gathering of believers that I do not seem to be able to experience alone or with friends. Although I believe that much of our spiritual growth takes place on our own through prayer, meditation, reading, and other means, there are certain things that we can experience only in larger gatherings. We cannot, for example, experience community on our own.

In larger gatherings such as church meetings and conferences, I have picked up a passion and excitement for the Lord that has kept me going for months. I have heard people speak negatively of such experiences, describing them as "camp fever." But I think the excitement that we come home with after a meeting or conference is a perfectly healthy and natural part of our Christian walk. We sometimes forget that life has rhythms and seasons. Sometimes we are excited and passionate about things and other times we are in more of a lull. Moments of passion sometimes keep us going when we have been experiencing tougher periods.

One reason we can experience a real high after a church meeting or conference is the impartation that can take place between people. This is biblical.

> For I long to see you, that I may impart to you some spiritual gift, to the end that you may be established. (Rom. 1:11)

> Don't neglect the gift that is in you, which was given to you by prophecy, with the laying on of the hands of the elders. (1 Tim. 4:14)

> For this cause, I remind you that you should stir up the gift of God which is in you through the laying on of my hands. (2 Tim. 1:6)

These verses show us that other believers, especially elders, can impart a gift to us. I am not implying that God cannot touch our lives *without* the help of others, but there seems to be something special about receiving a blessing from others.

Another passage, Psalm 133, hints at an anointing that can flow in a united gathering:

> See how good and how pleasant it is for brothers to live together in unity! It is like the precious oil on the head, that ran down on the beard, even Aaron's beard; that came down on the edge of his robes; like the dew of Hermon, that comes down on the hills of Zion: for there Yahweh gives the blessing, even life forevermore.

The oil in this passage symbolizes the Holy Spirit's presence among those who gather in unity. This is a promise of blessing to those living together in unity.

Encountering Difficult Circumstances

James encourages Christians not to be put off by the trials of life but to allow them to do their work in us.

> Count it all joy, my brothers, when you fall into various temptations, knowing that the testing of your faith produces endurance. Let endurance have its perfect work, that you may be perfect and complete, lacking in nothing. (James 1:2–4)

This is easier said than done. We have all been through difficult times that we hated during the process but, once we were safely out the other end, could look back on and see how much growth had taken place in our lives. These times are a gift from God. Even Jesus, our master, learned obedience through the things he suffered. "Though he was a Son, yet learned obedience by the things which he suffered" (Heb. 5:8).

As I said before, discipleship is about learning obedience and becoming like Christ. We therefore cannot escape the fact that God will allow us, his children, to go through difficult circumstances that will further shape us into his image. This is part of his loving discipline.

At times in my Christian walk, God has helped me learn humility in pretty tough ways. I don't look back on these situations with the fondest memories, because they were tough times, but I am thankful for the lessons the Lord taught me in the midst of them. On one particular occasion I remember thinking that I was some kind of expert at hearing from God and in my arrogance ignored common sense and the gentle warnings of the Spirit. I went headlong into a situation that caused me serious embarrassment. The situation involved a girl and talk of romance, but I shall say no more. Although this was a painful experience (even today I wince at the thought of meeting this girl again), I learned some precious lessons about humility, hearing from God, and obedience. These lessons are still with me today and have probably prevented even bigger disasters than that one.

My hope is that in this chapter I have persuaded you even just a little bit to look beyond traditional views of discipleship and spiritual growth and take hold of the many sources of growth that God has given us. My list is by no means exhaustive. It is merely meant to open your eyes to possibilities around you. The life of Christ flows in some unusual places, and we must try to make the most of this.

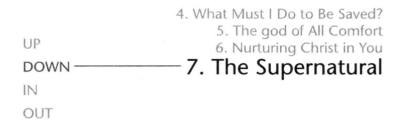

4. What Must I Do to Be Saved?
5. The god of All Comfort
UP
6. Nurturing Christ in You
DOWN ——————— **7. The Supernatural**
IN
OUT

The area of the supernatural has been a challenge to my faith since I have lived in the Western world. If the Bible is true, then shouldn't we expect to see a lot more supernatural occurrences? Personally, I have been learning to expect supernatural events and miracles, but it seems to me that many people do not share this expectation.

Back Home

In Sierra Leone the supernatural is actually very natural. People talk about it in everyday conversation. There are all kinds of secret societies that do weird and wonderful things. For example, one secret society has some kind of masked dancer, or so it seems. This entity can grow to the height of a two-story building and shrink as low as a couple of feet, and it can be summoned. The people strike the ground a few times, and out it comes. These apparent masked dancers from secret societies are aptly called devils back home. There is another group who are famous for having a man mutilate himself by removing eyes or ears or

125

cutting his tongue but later return whole. My favorite story was in a local paper about how a particular woman had gone to the US in a peanut shell to cast spells on some other woman.

The culture has many stories and parables, all containing the supernatural, and people accept this as normal. People visit witch doctors to find cures for diseases or get the right job or marriage partner. In rituals to celebrate the death of a relative, people leave food out for the dead. Interestingly, people tend to have some form of interaction with the supernatural regardless of what religion they claim to be a part of. Muslims consult witch doctors, and people calling themselves Christians gladly communicate with the dead and pour libation on the ground. Growing up, my family always had something going on with some dead relative somewhere that required us to do something. All these things are part of everyday life. No one ever questions whether they achieve anything. Nobody asks, for example, why the food left out for a dead relative is still there in the morning.

The naturalness of the supernatural does not stop with the culture. It also affects the way Christians in Sierra Leone live out their faith. When people become part of the church, they do not leave their belief in the supernatural behind; rather, they change allegiances. From being involved in the dark side of the supernatural, they now walk in the light of Christ.

The effects of prayer are real to many people. My mother, who is very much an intercessor, had a young woman as a prayer partner who could see what was going on in the spirit world as they prayed.

Dreams are also important. Within twenty-four hours of making one of my earliest commitments to Christ, I received a prophetic dream from the Lord. My mum helped me recognize the significance of the dream. Another example is when my mum had a dream in which she consciously battled with a woman she knew. In the dream experience, my mum was able to overpower the woman through the authority of Christ. The weird thing was that my mum saw the woman the next day, and they discussed the previous night. The woman was curious as to how my mum was able to overpower her, and my mum took that opportunity to share the gospel with her.

The reality of witches and the like trying to bring harm to the church is also something that comes up. It is not uncommon for someone who has been attending a church for a little while to confess to being an agent for a witch's coven and share some of the things they have been up to—how they seduce pastors to crush their ministries and how they try to harm church members.

Such events may sound far-fetched and ridiculous to Westerners. But they are not only true; they are a regular occurrence among many Christians in Sierra Leone.

Worldview and Expectation

I believe that the reason so many supernatural things occur in some cultures but not in others is that some cultures expect them to occur and others do not. Another way of saying it is that some cultures have faith for these things. People in these cultures do not know any differently; the supernatural has always been real to them.

There is a Bible passage that talks about Jesus not being able to do any major miracle in a particular town.

Jesus went out from there and came into His hometown; and His disciples followed Him. When the Sabbath came,

He began to teach in the synagogue; and the many lis-
teners were astonished, saying, "Where did this man get
these things, and what is this wisdom given to Him, and
such miracles as these performed by His hands? Is not this
the carpenter, the son of Mary, and brother of James and
Joses and Judas and Simon? Are not His sisters here with
us?" And they took offense at Him. Jesus said to them, "A
prophet is not without honor except in his hometown and
among his own relatives and in his own household." And
He could do no miracle there except that He laid His hands
on a few sick people and healed them. And He wondered at
their unbelief. (Mark 6:1–6 NASB)

This passage supports my belief that the supernatural occurs
where it is expected but is not likely to occur where it is not
expected.

Expectation can come from many sources within our cultures, and it can also come from God. For example, if God
wants to heal someone and tells that to someone else who is
praying for that person, the pray-er's faith will rise; he or she
will begin to expect the healing, and then the healing will occur.
Even then, certain cultures are more likely to expect God to tell
people to pray for a healing.

In short, I would say that some cultures are fortunate enough
to have a worldview that accepts the supernatural, whereas other
cultures have drifted into a more reductionist worldview. We can
spend a lot of time berating one another for a lack of miracles
in the Western church, but that won't help. What we really need
is to come to a place of renewing our minds so that we adopt a
more biblical worldview rather than the prevalent worldview of
the culture. I will explain what I mean by this.

Modern Worldview

In the Western world the predominant worldview has been a
modern worldview. Within this worldview the emphasis is on
"seeing is believing." If you can't feel it, touch it, dissect it, and
take it apart, then it cannot be real. The level of atheism and
agnosticism in the UK today is not surprising considering the
way we have embraced modern thinking. For example, if you
teach children from a young age that God did not create the
world but that the world was formed by accident, then not only
will most of the kids not believe in God, but the few who might
believe in God are highly unlikely to expect him to intervene in
the world.

Many Western Christians think they strongly believe in the
supernatural. If you look at the way most of us live our lives,
however, you will realize that our behavior does not reflect this
"strong belief" that we may claim to have. Here is a simple test
for you. This is an easy question requiring a quick answer:

If you have a headache, what do you do?

The common answers are: drink water and/or take a pill.

You might think a headache is trivial. In that case let me
generalize and ask a different question:

If you are sick, what is the first thing you think of doing
about it?

The most common answer is: go to the doctor.

This is not a criticism but merely an observation. Our
answers are the natural result of living in a modern world, where
science and knowledge are king. We rely on medicine to the
point that even when problems find their origin in something
clearly not biological, we still sometimes use drugs. For example,
some mental illnesses, such as depression, are a result of adverse

circumstances such as bereavement, yet in some cases doctors prescribe drugs rather than let grief take its course.

Postmodern Worldview

There is good news, however, for the younger generation. It seems that the move into postmodernity has brought with it a greater appreciation of the supernatural. Psychic and New Age fairs are springing up all over the place with growing numbers of attenders each time. Many people today believe in the supernatural and have even experienced it. I sometimes do a survey to get a feel for a place that I visit. One of the questions I ask people is, "Have you ever had any supernatural experiences?" It is amazing how many people will respond affirmatively to that question. This shows that some people are now drifting away from the modern way of looking at the world to the postmodern way, which makes room for the supernatural.

I recently went to a body-and-soul fair with some friends to pray and intercede for those at the fair and see whether God would give us any opportunities for sharing our faith. I was fascinated by all the different stalls. In addition to the usual clairvoyants, there were a few stalls focused on healing. There was reiki healing, shiatsu massage, and an Egyptian-based treatment that involved a man standing over his client with arms in the air and calling upon a greater power. There were also lectures about finding out your secret name and the name of your angel. Lots of people came and went, picked up readings, and attended sessions focused on healing and predictions. This might not have been a mainstream group of people, but these people certainly reflect something of where our postmodern world is at right now or where it may be headed.

The reality is that people would like to experience some of this supernatural stuff before they listen to our message about Jesus. Some Christians were running an Alpha Course in South East Asia and found that they needed to do the Holy Spirit Weekend first—before they did the lectures. In the Alpha manual the Holy Spirit Weekend normally comes toward the end of the course, but the people were so hungry for and expectant of the supernatural that had they not experienced it early on in the course, they would have lost interest. This might seem strange to some people, but it doesn't seem strange to me. I would even dare say that it wouldn't seem strange to Jesus either. On more than one occasion he healed people first before leading them to faith. My favorite example of this has to be the story about the blind man receiving his sight.

> As he passed by, he saw a man blind from birth. His disciples asked him, "Rabbi, who sinned, this man or his parents, that he was born blind?"
>
> Jesus answered, "Neither did this man sin, nor his parents; but, that the works of God might be revealed in him. I must work the works of him who sent me, while it is day. The night is coming, when no one can work. While I am in the world, I am the light of the world." When he had said this, he spat on the ground, made mud with the saliva, anointed the blind man's eyes with the mud, and said to him, "Go, wash in the pool of Siloam" (which means "Sent"). So he went away, washed, and came back seeing.
>
> ...Jesus heard that they had thrown him out, and finding him, he said, "Do you believe in the Son of God?"
>
> He answered, "Who is he, Lord, that I may believe in him?"

UP

DOWN

IN

OUT

Jesus said to him, "You have both seen him, and it is he who speaks with you."

He said, "Lord, I believe!" and he worshiped him. (John 9:1–7, 35–38)

In this story, the blind man was open to the supernatural, and eventually, after he was healed, he worked out who Jesus was and worshiped him. I do not think it is unreasonable to expect similar things to occur in our time, but we must first learn to be open to the supernatural.

The Bible and the Supernatural

The Bible speaks naturally about the supernatural. It talks about miracles in the same way we would talk about nipping down to the shops. I love the verse that says, "Enoch walked with God, and he was not, for God took him" (Gen 5:24). Or take the fact that Elijah was taken up in a chariot of fire. The Bible talks about God and his supernatural acts without even attempting to explain in any way how these things happen, not to mention how God came into being. It makes many references to God telling someone to do something—again with little in the way of explanation as to how exactly God spoke to the person. It also refers to supernatural beings created by God. Some verses refer to angels doing the Lord's work, and some refer to demonic activity.

I once went through the book of Genesis and counted how many chapters had something supernatural going on. I found that apart from just a handful of chapters, every chapter had something supernatural in it. In just the first few chapters you have creation, a talking snake, and sons of God coming and having children with the daughters of men, to name a few. John Paul Jackson shared at a conference that over a third of the Bible relates to dreams, visions, and prophetic utterances from God. When you throw in miraculous events as well, then a vast amount of the Bible is related to the supernatural.

Jesus and the Supernatural

If there was anyone who demonstrated how natural it is to be supernatural, it was Jesus. Many stories of Jesus engage in the supernatural and make no apology or excuses for it. Jesus' conception was surrounded by mysterious and supernatural events that were so out there that many people, including professing Christians, struggle to believe that Jesus' mother was a virgin, that Jesus was born in a stable and angels announced his birth to shepherds, and that a star guided some wise men to Bethlehem. All very trippy, I think.

Jesus then lived a life that was marked with other supernatural events. His ministry commenced with a voice speaking from heaven and a dove landing on his head. Jesus was then driven by the Holy Spirit out into the desert, where he fasted and the devil appeared to him, making some generous offers. If these events occurred within the modern context, they would be seen as incredibly bizarre. Anyone insisting that the devil appeared to him or her would likely be institutionalized, but such supernatural occurrences took place in the life of Christ. Here are some more examples.

Not only did Jesus go around healing blind people and lame people, but he talked to demons and kicked them out of people. At another point Jesus was sound asleep on a boat while it and the crew were on the edge of disaster; he then woke up and told the wind and waves where to go, and they obeyed him. To me these kinds of things smack of the unusual. And as if you needed further convincing, I will carry on.

Jesus was spending time with his disciples and led them up to a high mountain. Suddenly two prominent prophets from Israel's past appeared to the men, Jesus' clothes turned extremely white, and Jesus held a conversation with the two prophets. And how does someone like this face a wrongful trial? With relative calm and dignity because he knew what lay ahead. Not only did he actually rise from the dead, but during the time that he was still on earth after his resurrection, he appeared inside a room with closed doors and could make himself unrecognizable to his disciples. He rounded up the whole thing by floating into the heavens to be with his Father.

There really is never a dull moment with Jesus. We must face the fact that the supernatural is real. I once heard someone say that the unseen, spiritual world is more real than the seen, physical world. The Bible puts it another, better way: what is seen is temporal but what is unseen is eternal (2 Cor. 4:18). For me there is a greater sense of reality with the eternal, spiritual world.

Angels

It seems from the Scriptures that behind supernatural events are spiritual beings. The Bible talks about God's messengers, or angels as we call them. The Greek word translated "angel" simply means "messenger" and can be used to refer to human or non-human messengers. However, the word is used mostly to refer to the spirits God has created to serve him and his purposes. These beings are very much present in the Bible and again no apologies, explanations, or excuses are offered for them; they are just talked about. Angels make their appearances in many significant stories from Genesis to Revelation. From the angels who guarded the entrance to the Garden of Eden to the angel who blows the last trumpet in Revelation, the Bible is full of them.

Angels seem to make an appearance at crucial times to serve a specific purpose. Most angels are not mentioned by name, but a few angels are. For example, the angel Gabriel acted as some kind of messenger who turned up and spoke to Daniel on two occasions (Dan. 8:16; 9:21). It was Gabriel who told Mary about the birth of Christ (Luke 1:26). Also mentioned by name is Michael. In the book of Daniel, Michael is described as a chief prince who came to the aid of Gabriel and fought with the prince of Persia (Dan. 10:13). He is also seen contending with the devil for the body of Moses (Jude 1:9). Finally, he is seen as a warrior angel fighting on behalf of God (Rev. 12:7).

The fact that angels are mentioned in the Bible and that we are told the names of two of them shows that angels are part of biblical reality. Whether or not we realize it, angels are busy working in this world on behalf of God. Sometimes they make themselves visible and sometimes not. I have known more than one person who has been able to see angels. These people have spoken of the fact that there is always at least one angel around us.

Although the Bible indicates that angels are not to be worshiped (Col. 2:18; Rev. 22:8–9), it does not ask us to ignore them or pretend they are not there. I am grateful to God for the fact that angels exist and that they have at times come to our aid and our protection as the Lord has commanded, both in biblical times and the present. We have a supernatural God who uses supernatural beings to accomplish supernatural purposes.

Demons

Another angel specifically referred to in the Bible is the angel who leads an army of rebel angels (sometimes called demons) who have chosen no longer to serve their creator God. This angel is many times called Satan, the devil, the serpent, or the adversary. If read symbolically, Isaiah indicates that his former name, before he chose to rebel against God, was Lucifer (Isa. 14:12 KJV). The Bible speaks openly about Satan and demons, and Jesus spent a major part of his ministry confronting them. At times the Bible identifies demons by the work they do—for example, a lying spirit (1 Kings 22:22) and a spirit of divination (Acts 16:16).

Many Westerners find it hard to accept the existence of Satan and demons and the possibility of them influencing the lives of humans, yet many cultures around the world do recognize that evil spirits are out there seeking to cause harm. Within these cultures you will find ceremonies or talismans designed to keep evil at bay. Convincing such people of the existence of demons is not at all necessary; they are already familiar with them. Demons can have effects—such as sickness, disease, death, apparent insanity, and a whole host of other things—on our physical world. They are also involved in appropriating curses that, for example, a witch doctor might have spoken out against a person. We do not know much about demons, but we know that for some reason they desire to occupy space in our lives and even our bodies if given the chance.

All these examples show us that demons are a reality and are actively involved in influencing our world. But some people prefer to believe that there are no such things as demons or evil spirits. They prefer to think that Satan is just a made-up person in the Bible to convey the concept of evil. In my opinion, however, the Bible is literal in its references to Satan and his cohorts.

Warfare

The reality that Satan and his followers exist leads us to the conclusion that a war is going on in the unseen spiritual realm. "There was war in the sky. Michael and his angels made war on the dragon. The dragon and his angels made war" (Rev. 12:7). In this verse we see that one of God's archangels and the dragon (the devil) are locked in battle. Although this battle is one specific instance, it is actually a culmination of many battles that have taken place and that will take place between God's army of light and Satan's army of darkness.

God and Satan have very different agendas. Satan desires to kill, steal, and destroy in our world, but God desires to enliven, bless, and create. While Satan goes around doing his work, so does God. They war against each other's agendas. The Scriptures show, however, that this is not an equal fight that will rage on for eternity. Christ has already won the battle on the Cross, and this victory comes into effect as God's will is done on earth and will find its ultimate fulfillment at the end of the world as we know it (Rev. 20:10; 1 Cor. 15:57).

John writes in his first letter that the purpose of Christ being revealed was to destroy the works of the enemy (1 John 3:8). The Cross has made possible the destruction of the devil's work, but this is yet to be fully implemented. And this is where we come in. John 20:21 says, "As the Father has sent me, even so I send you." We have been called to engage in the supernatural work of destroying the works of the enemy. It is a tragedy that we so readily abandon our call because of unbelief and an adherence to apparent cultural norms that are not norms at all. Let's look at some aspects of our call.

Healing

We are called to be involved in supernatural healing of both physical and nonphysical ailments. This was a major part of Jesus' work on earth and is meant to be part of the work of the church of Jesus Christ. Many people would like to believe that supernatural healing does not occur. Some say it used to take place but doesn't happen anymore. There is, however, no evidence in the Bible to suggest that healing does not take place anymore, and my personal experience backs this up. I have seen several people healed from different ailments, and I myself have experienced a healing that I cannot explain in any other way than that it came from a supernatural source, namely, God. Here's my story.

For the better part of a decade I was dependent on medication to reduce the amount of acid swirling around my stomach. The strength of drugs I needed to ease my discomfort had to be steadily increased until I was prescribed one of the strongest drugs available. I had had quite a few tests to work out the problem, but no real cause was known, except possibly stress. And since life is full of stressful situations, there seemed to be no hope for me. On several occasions I prayed and asked God to intervene and heal my stomach.

One night I had a dream that I took my regular pills and ended up feeling nauseous and bringing them back up. The dream was graphic and real, and I felt weird when I woke up. I started to pray and ask the Lord what this meant. It did not take long for me to realize that the time had come for my healing and that God wanted me to stop taking the pills. It took me a while to obey this dream, but eventually I did stop taking the pills. The first week was shaky as my stomach adjusted to the absence of the pills, so once I took some lower strength pills. But within a week all discomfort was gone, and I had no pain at all. After nearly a decade of dependence on pharmaceuticals I no longer need them for my stomach. It took a while for my prayers to be answered, but when they were, I was left with no doubt that God was involved. God is indeed a supernatural God in the healing business today.

Because of this personal experience and the experiences of many people, I have an unshakeable belief in God's call to his church to administer supernatural healing to a broken and wounded world.

Casting Out Demons

It is sad enough that so many people are in bondage to evil spirits in our world, but what is even sadder is that we have all kinds of ways to describe their condition instead of facing the reality that some illnesses are influenced by evil spirits. If we don't make the right diagnosis, then we can't prescribe the right treatment.

In Denmark recently, a psychiatrist published a fictional book in which he suggested that some of the patients in an asylum were suffering from demonization. He was called in by his superiors and asked to deny that he held such beliefs. He refused to do so. As might be expected, he lost his job because the health service did not want him working with the patients if he held such beliefs.

Because of my degree in psychology, I know that biochemical disorders can cause mental illness. Therefore not every mental illness is due to demonization, but some of them are. There was a case where a man who had suffered from mental illness for years found freedom in Christ. The man had developed the problem of hearing voices after a lifestyle in which he abused drugs. This problem had gone on for years until he attended a healing retreat where the voices were cast out in the name of Jesus and healing came. Later the man expressed frustration that no one had helped him consider that the origin of his problem was spiritual. He was grieved for other people he knew who had mental problems that doctors and the like were not able to treat. Since he found his freedom, he has tried to help others find theirs through prayer.

Many people around us suffering from mental, physical, or emotional problems are demonized and need the supernatural power of God to set them free.

Called to Be Supernatural

If our goal as Christians is to do the works of God and to live as Christ did, then we must begin to allow God to open us up to supernatural things. For me the question of whether the supernatural exists has not been a problem. The questions in my mind have been whether I am called to be involved in supernatural acts, whether I have access to supernatural power, and if so, how I am supposed to use such access.

God is a spiritual being who does unexplainable things in our world. The Bible is clear that as Christians we are born of his Spirit, not of a natural birth (see John 3:3–6). It makes sense that a supernatural God who does supernatural things will have children who also can (and should) engage in the supernatural.

As Christians we desire truth and reality. The truth and reality is that we live in a world that is impacted by supernatural beings. We have a choice: to engage in the supernatural and be able to influence our world, or to passively be affected by the supernatural. If we think we can sit on the sidelines and be mere observers, we are wrong. That choice is not available to us. We must decide whether to be active or passive in the area of the supernatural.

UP

DOWN

IN

OUT

Section C

Look IN to the church

8. What Is Church, Anyway?

What is church? Many people at different times have come up with all sorts of answers to this question.

In my Christian walk I never thought to ask this question until people started preaching about new expressions of church. I thought I knew what church was, and that was that. I knew that I had encountered good churches and bad churches, but I had never questioned whether some of my bad church experiences could even be called genuine church experiences. However, God has his ways of bringing up such questions when we least expect it. When God posed the question, what is church? to me, I thought it was an easy one. I am sure you are familiar with God asking questions that are not straightforward. He is usually trying to teach us something; he asks us questions not so that he can hear our answers but so that *we* can hear our answers and our own hearts. Suffice it to say that my search for an answer to the question, what is church? began an extraordinary journey into my Bible.

As I attempted to answer this question, I felt God speak something that revealed my heart. For me church was about getting together on a Sunday and singing songs passionately with several hundred watts of PA. This was followed by the collection and notices, and then finally we arrived at the main event we had all been waiting for: a stirring sermon by the preacher of the day. But God had some different ideas. He pointed out that my definition of church excluded, for example, the persecuted church in China. My view of church included loud worship with a rock band, but this would be unheard of in the underground church of China. Loud meetings in China would invite the unwanted attention of the secret police who would be only too happy to find a large gathering of Christians.

So why did my definition of the church exclude the church in China? Because it was based on my limited experience of church rather than what the Bible says about it. My limited experience had blinded me to what the Scriptures say about church. In this chapter I want to share some of the ideas I have and conclusions I've drawn about church over the past few years.

The Organization We Call Church

Many of us are quickly taught after becoming Christians that church is not the building but the people. This truth is something that rolls off our tongues so fast that I'm not sure it ever hits our hearts. Not only do many of us still refer to buildings as churches, but more disappointing is the fact that we have yet to grasp the implications and apply the truth that church is the people. Although people may recognize that church is not the building, some think of church as a meeting or some kind of organization to be a part of. I recall reading an article by Chip Brogden (of www.theschoolofchrist.org) in which he described some people's attitude toward church as a kind of organization:

the members have a shared interest and so rent or buy a building to express this interest and hire people to help them administer things.

Many church groups resemble large corporations. There is a CEO (the pastor). There are shareholders (the congregation). There is a board of directors (elders). There are products such as books, sermons, and tapes. And they hold regular meetings and conferences (church gatherings and worship concerts).

When we begin to look deep into what church is, we may realize that although some of what we are being and doing is not morally wrong, it is a fair distance away from what was called "church" in the New Testament.

Defining Ecclesia

As you may imagine, after becoming aware that my definition of church excluded some precious saints in the world, I had to identify where I had gone wrong and attempt to discover what God meant by church.

Sometimes I get a shock about my thinking that is difficult to take. For example, when I learned how few times the word *Christian* is found in the Bible, I was horrified. This word that I had so identified myself with was never used by Jesus. In fact, scholars say that it was a mocking term for followers of Jesus meaning "little Christs," or in another sense, "Wannabe Jesuses." The image of Mini-Me in *Austin Powers* comes to mind when I think of "little Christ"—or should I say, "Mini-Christ"? In the same way, I was surprised to find that the word *church* was used only twice by Jesus and that although this word is used many times later on in the New Testament, it was used differently from the way I had used it for a long time.

147

The first time we find the word that we translate "church" in the Bible is in Matthew 16. "I also tell you that you are Peter, and on this rock I will build my assembly, and the gates of Hades will not prevail against it" (Matt. 16:18). You will notice that the word *church* does not appear in this verse at all. That is because I am using the World English Bible (WEB), and this version never features the word *church*. I find this helpful because *church* conjures up the wrong images for us. In order to get the real sense of the meaning of the Greek word, it is better to translate it as "assembly."

The Greek word I am talking about is one you are probably familiar with. It is *ecclesia*. Scholars say that one of the best ways to translate this word is "called-out ones." An ecclesia is a group of people called out from among a larger group. Like many words found in the New Testament, this word was used in everyday conversation and was later adapted to mean something more specific, namely, *Jesus'* called-out ones. As followers of Christ we have been called out from the world, from our former lives, into a new way of living in relationship with our Creator.

I do not want to attempt a deep study into the meaning of the word *ecclesia* because neither am I qualified nor is it necessary for our purposes here. My main point at this stage is to emphasize that ecclesia specifically refers to people. It never refers to buildings or meetings. We are therefore mistaken when we refer to gatherings of the church as church itself.

The First Ecclesia

Another surprise came when I learned that the concept of ecclesia did not originate in the New Testament. If we open up our minds to the simpler and broader understanding of church as people, we see that the first church was the people of Israel. In

his parting words recorded in Acts 7, Stephen recounts a summarized history of Israel and their relationship with God. I want
to make a specific observation about one verse in this speech,
Acts 7:38. Let's look at two versions of this verse:

> This is he who was in the assembly in the wilderness with
> the angel that spoke to him on Mount Sinai, and with our
> fathers, who received living oracles to give to us. (WEB)

> This is he, that was in the church in the wilderness with
> the angel which spake to him in the mount Sina, and with
> our fathers: who received the lively oracles to give unto us.
> (KJV)

The King James Version uses the word *church* to be con-
sistent with its use of the word so far. Therefore the concept
of church was conceived not after the death, resurrection, and
ascension of Jesus but when God first *called out* the nation of
Israel. Again, I want to encourage us to broaden our definition
of church so that we don't exclude other Christians in God's
community of people who are precious to him (not that we
could actually exclude anyone by our own narrow-mindedness,
since only God has the right to declare who is part of his church).
God has always had his chosen community. Before it was those
who entered into a covenant with Yahweh (i.e., Israel), but now
it is those who belong to the covenant community of Christ.
Christians have a terrible history of persecuting one another
when others do not fit neatly into the boxes in our minds of
what the church is.

Changing our definition of church will have far-reaching
effects. For example, many people are talking about church
planting today, but what does that really mean? If we do not

UP

DOWN

IN

OUT

know what churches are, how can we plant them? Are we going to acquire buildings or organize meetings? Do we simply aim to make disciples of Jesus who will then naturally be incorporated into the body of Christ? These are not easy questions to answer but are well worth exploring.

Learning from Missionaries and Other Cultures

In my quest to answer difficult questions like, what is church? and, how do we join Christ in expanding his church?, I have delved into many sources and learned from a variety of people. Some of the most precious lessons I have learned came from those who are at the forefront of expanding the kingdom all over the world and are working in some pretty unfriendly places. As I explored the teachings of missionaries and looked at the methods they have used to reach some of the most resistant people groups with the gospel, I came to believe that our missionaries are some of the most underused resources in the body of Christ. It seems as if what they have to say and do is good enough for the "natives" of some far-flung nation but is not good enough for us back home.

It also seems as if the methods used by the underground church in China to meet and grow in faith are second best and that we in the West have the ideal that the other nations should strive to achieve. I know that this is not true, but sadly many churches around the world, in places like West Africa, for example, look to the UK and US churches as the model of what church should be like. This is a tragedy, because many of these nations have greater insights about life in the kingdom of God than we do in the West. What if the underground church is actually the ideal of what the church should be like and we in the

West are the ones who have second best? I think this is closer to the truth than any of us would like to admit.

Why do I say this? I believe that the body of Christ is exactly that—a body. A body is a living organism, and all living organisms grow. You can even measure the health of a living organism by how much it grows. It is a well-accepted fact that the fastest growing churches in the world are in developing nations, not in the West. Some researchers believe that the church in Europe is actually in decline. A few segments of the church are growing (for example, black churches in London), but many more are shrinking. On the other hand, some figures suggest that the church in China is growing by ten thousand people per day. We should ask ourselves why this is the case. If we want even to glimpse that kind of growth in the West, we will have to start taking our missionaries who are effectively planting churches around the world more seriously. We will have to take poorer and less educated nations more seriously too, because they are displaying more growth than we are.

Ten Universal Elements

Many studies have been done to see what elements are present in churches around the world that are experiencing significant growth. One such study is contained in a booklet called *Church Planting Movements* by David Garrison. Garrison notes some key elements involved in a specific type of church growth, which he calls a church planting movement. You will have to forgive me for devoting so much space in my book to another book, but I believe this is a significant work.

Let's start by gaining a broad understanding of such a movement. Garrison writes, "A simple, concise definition of a Church

Planting Movement (CPM) is a rapid and multiplicative increase of indigenous churches planting churches within a given people group or population segment." The key words to observe in this definition are:

- Rapid—growth occurs over a relatively short period of time
- Multiplicative—numbers increase exponentially (1 to 2; 2 to 4; 4 to 8; etc.)
- Indigenous—new churches are started by and consist of local people, not outsiders

Garrison observed that specific elements were present whenever a church planting movement was found among a people group. He describes these as the "Ten Universal Elements of a CPM." Although I will not go into great detail, it is worth quickly examining these ten elements of every CPM.

Prayer. At the heart of every movement of God, whether it be church planting, revival, or Alpha, there has always been an emphasis on prayer.

Abundant gospel sowing. According to Romans 10, for people to be saved the gospel must be preached. Simple logic suggests that if the gospel isn't preached, people won't come to Christ; and if the gospel is preached abundantly, many people will likely come to Christ.

Intentional church planting. Church planting does not happen accidentally, or if it does, it is unlikely to survive. In successful CPMs, strategy is in place before they begin.

Scriptural authority. The unquestioned authority of the Bible is important for a CPM. Opinion, culture, popular vote, and tradition all bow to the authority of Scripture. This is important so that we can have an objective, universal starting point upon which we all agree. Without this we would descend into chaos and heresy.

Local leadership. After their vital work of getting things going, the missionaries take a backseat role and allow locals to lead the movement. This requires much discipline on the missionaries' part.

Lay leadership. In order to have a large number of church planters and leaders available, a church planting movement is primarily led by lay people who reflect the people they are leading.

Cell or house churches. Cell churches are usually a network of small churches organized under a single authority, whereas house churches are small, independent churches with their own leadership structure. The advantage of both of these kinds of churches is that they do not require buildings and therefore allow for rapid multiplication.

Churches planting churches. Although initial churches are planted by missionaries or other trained church planters, there comes a point when the churches themselves begin to plant churches. At this stage the movement can reach a multiplicative growth phase because church planting is not restricted by the number of missionaries or trained church planters.

Rapid reproduction. Although some people argue that this is a fruit of a CPM rather than a requirement, many church planters have found that rapid reproduction causes Christians to carry an urgency for the gospel and prevents them from becoming occupied with the nonessentials of the faith (which often distract us in the West from getting on with kingdom business).

Healthy churches. Church growth experts agree on five elements that need to be present for a church to be considered

healthy: worship, evangelistic and missionary outreach, education and discipleship, ministry, and fellowship. When each of
these is present in a church, growth is the natural result.

Simplicity of Church

As I look at these ten universal elements, the word that comes to
mind is *simplicity*. Nothing within these elements is so complex
that only a few churches could apply them. I believe that this is
one of the areas in which the Western church has lost its way.
We have some complex and resource-demanding ways of being
church. For example, I was once told about a denomination that
required every church planter to raise a million dollars to plant
a church, because that is what the leaders of the denomination
estimated it would cost to do so. Such requirements slow down
the growth of our churches. It's simple mathematics. If church
planting requires a million dollars, then we can only plant a
church when we have raised that amount. For some churches,
that could take years, for others decades, for still others—they
will never plant a church.

I also want to draw your attention to local and lay leadership. Again, we have made leadership complex for no good
reason and are in danger of completely missing the point. In the
New Testament the emphasis for leadership is on character and
obedience. In his letters to Titus and Timothy, Paul highlights
requirements for leadership in the church that are very different from our requirements. We require people to have degrees
to be leaders. It seems to matter little what their reputation is
or whether they are lovers of money so long as they have been
to Bible school or seminary. I am not against good Bible or
leadership training; however, I feel the balance leans too much

toward formal training and not enough on godly enabling and character. Again, this is a bottleneck for growth because of the time it takes to study and also the costs involved. There are very anointed and highly capable leaders out there who will never be church leaders if we adhere to these standards because they lack finances or access to formal training.

I have come to believe that the key to a fruitful church is biblical simplicity. We must not add complexities to church. At the heart of being church is simply the fact that we have been called out by Christ, who is at the center of our community, and we seek to obey him and all that he has commanded us to do. It has always amazed me that Jesus said we would be known as his disciples by the way we love one another (John 13:35). Church involves the simplicity of loving one another and not many of the complex extras and traditions that we have added. It takes real objectivity to be able to discern which aspects of being church are biblical, which are cultural, and which are traditional. It requires honesty to recognize where we have put our traditions above the Word of God and have therefore excluded others or failed to fulfill our duties.

We must heed the warning of Jesus that we can hold on to traditions instead of his commands.

> He answered them, "Well did Isaiah prophesy of you hypocrites, as it is written, 'This people honors me with their lips, but their heart is far from me. But in vain do they worship me, teaching as doctrines the commandments of men.' For you set aside the commandment of God, and hold tightly to the tradition of men—the washing of pitchers and cups, and you do many other such things." He said to them, "Full well do you reject the commandment of God, that you may

keep your tradition. For Moses said, 'Honor your father and your mother;' and, 'He who speaks evil of father or mother, let him be put to death.' But you say, 'If a man tells his father or his mother, "Whatever profit you might have received from me is Corban, that is to say, given to God;"' then you no longer allow him to do anything for his father or his mother, making void the word of God by your tradition, which you have handed down. You do many things like this." (Mark 7:6–13)

Jesus highlights that we hold on to tradition even at the expense of caring for others, and in this case, our parents.

Again, we must learn from our missionary friends who, finding themselves in rather unusual circumstances, have been forced to distill the core commands of Christ. When it comes down to it, we are called to obey Jesus, and anyone who believes and obeys Jesus can be said to be a part of his church.

Commands of Jesus

In their *Church Multiplication Guide*, George Patterson and Richard Scoggins helpfully distinguish between New Testament commands and other traditions. To do this they discuss levels of authority.

The first level of authority to which we are to submit is the commands of Jesus. These are the non-negotiables that we must obey and must encourage others to obey and not hinder them from obeying. The next level is apostolic practices, which are practices not explicitly commanded in the New Testament but which we observe the apostles doing. For example, many times in the New Testament people were baptized soon after conversion (such as Philip and the eunuch in Acts 8:35–38). This is probably a good thing to do but is not explicitly commanded. It is therefore a good idea to engage in these practices when we can, but we cannot hold them as non-negotiables and should never allow them to divide the body of Christ. The final level is human customs. These are fine and good as long as they do not prevent the obedience of the first-level commands of Jesus.

Many times in our churches we have failed to make these distinctions and to recognize the hierarchy that exists in our practices. We need to look closely at the first level of authority, the commands of Jesus. Patterson and Scoggins sum up these commands in seven broad categories:

Repent, believe, and receive the Holy Spirit

The time is fulfilled, and the Kingdom of God is at hand! Repent, and believe in the Good News. (Mark 1:15)

Jesus therefore said to them again, "Peace be to you. As the Father has sent me, even so I send you." When he had said this, he breathed on them, and said to them, "Receive the Holy Spirit! If you forgive anyone's sins, they have been forgiven them. If you retain anyone's sins, they have been retained" (John 20:21–23)

Baptize

Jesus came to them and spoke to them, saying, "All authority has been given to me in heaven and on earth. Go, and make disciples of all nations, baptizing them in the name of the Father and of the Son and of the Holy Spirit, teaching them to observe all things that I commanded you. Behold, I am with you always, even to the end of the age." Amen. (Matt. 28:18–20)

Break bread in remembrance of Jesus' death (Communion)

As they were eating, Jesus took bread, gave thanks for it, and broke it. He gave to the disciples, and said, "Take, eat; this is my body." He took the cup, gave thanks, and gave to them, saying, "All of you drink it, for this is my blood of the new covenant, which is poured out for many for the remission of sins." (Matt. 26:26–28)

For I received from the Lord that which also I delivered to you, that the Lord Jesus on the night in which he was betrayed took bread. When he had given thanks, he broke it, and said, "Take, eat. This is my body, which is broken for you. Do this in memory of me." In the same way he also took the cup, after supper, saying, "This cup is the new covenant in my blood. Do this, as often as you drink, in memory of me." (1 Cor. 11:23–25)

Love (God, others, even enemies)

When the multitudes heard it, they were astonished at his teaching. But the Pharisees, when they heard that he had silenced the Sadducees, gathered themselves together. One of them, a lawyer, asked him a question, testing him. "Teacher, which is the greatest commandment in the law?" Jesus said to him, "'You shall love the Lord your God with all your heart, with all your soul, and with all your mind.' This is the first and great commandment. A second likewise is this, 'You shall love your neighbor as yourself.' The whole law and the prophets depend on these two commandments." (Matt. 22:33–40)

But I tell you who hear: love your enemies, do good to those who hate you, bless those who curse you, and pray for those who mistreat you. To him who strikes you on the cheek, offer also the other; and from him who takes away your cloak, don't withhold your coat also. Give to everyone who asks you, and don't ask him who takes away your goods to give them back again. As you would like people to do to you, do exactly so to them. If you love those who love you, what credit is that to you? For even sinners love those who love them. If you do good to those who do good to you, what credit is that to you? For even sinners do the same. (Luke 6:27–33)

Pray

Until now, you have asked nothing in my name. Ask, and you will receive, that your joy may be made full. (John 16:24)

Give generously

Give, and it will be given to you: good measure, pressed down, shaken together, and running over, will be given to you. For with the same measure you measure it will be measured back to you. (Luke 6:38)

Make disciples

Jesus came to them and spoke to them, saying, "All authority has been given to me in heaven and on earth. Go, and make disciples of all nations, baptizing them in the name of the Father and of the Son and of the Holy Spirit, teaching them to observe all things that I commanded you. Behold, I am with you always, even to the end of the age." Amen. (Matt. 28:18–20)

This is not meant to be an extensive study of the commands of Jesus but is merely an introduction to whet your appetite and send you to the Bible to look for answers and more questions. Nevertheless, these commands carry the core of what we are supposed to be and do as the church of Jesus Christ.

It is tempting to add things that we think are important, such as some of the apostolic practices and human customs that we have developed over the years. George Patterson, in a document titled "Three Levels of Church Authority," encourages people to create a list of things that they consider to be a part of church and then divide the list into the three levels of authority. If you do this exercise, you will be surprised at what you find. For example, apostolic practices include meeting on Sundays and speaking in tongues. These may well be good practices that help Christians in their walk with God, but they are not explicitly commanded by Christ.

Human Customs and Historical Trends

We must recognize that many of our practices in church are based on human customs rather than the explicit commands of Jesus or even apostolic practices. Things that seem to us very much a part of church life have sometimes only existed for a couple of centuries or even decades. The reality is that culture and tradition will influence how we express our faith. For example, where I come from we love to dance, so dancing is a natural part of our worship. In many other traditions, however, dancing is actually frowned upon and considered to be "of the devil." To dance or not to dance is not an explicit command of Jesus, so it's not worth fighting over. But the reality is that for many people things such as dancing are contentious issues. Take also the issue of drinking. The Bible says we should not get drunk but never forbids drinking entirely. What is forbidden is drunkenness. It is important to remember that the church has adopted many practices that have a greater impact on us and the world than do issues such as dancing or drinking. For example, I am sometimes concerned by the lavish sanctuaries that some churches seem obsessed with building. The impact of such building projects is that not only does it reinforce the lie that it is important to worship in temples made with human hands, but we miss out on contributing toward other thing such as caring for widows and orphans or contributing to missions. We might first want to address the major issues before getting bogged down by the minor issues.

Many times what we consider to be an essential part of church and church gatherings is merely a trend that the church adopts for a season before another trend comes along. To illustrate this point, let me use an example from our church gatherings. If I were to ask you what item was most prominent in the front of the building during your gatherings, I would receive a number of different replies. These replies would be dependent on what denomination you are a part of and when that denomination was birthed.

It was common at one time (and is still this way in some traditions) for an altar to be at the front of the sanctuary, because the main event in the meeting was Communion, with all its mystery. Then as some churches moved into a more modern way of thinking where logic and argument were important, the sermon became the most important part of the meeting, and therefore the pulpit or lectern was put at the front of the sanctuary. In more recent times, with the growth of worship music and the emphasis on personal encounters with God through worship,

UP

DOWN

IN

OUT

some churches have opted to have the band and its instruments at the center of the room with a light and mobile lectern (or sometimes simply a music stand) brought up as necessary. Finally, with the impact of the move of the Holy Spirit in a fresh way, many churches have made ministry the center of their meetings and therefore no one item seems to dominate the front of the room. In this case, people often hurry through song-worship and Bible teaching to get to the main event: receiving prayer.

Going through these seasons and trends is a natural thing for any church. The reason why I bring it up is so that we realize that some of the things we treat as sacred cows are simply phases that the church is going through. Sometimes these phases are influenced by God, but at other times they are influenced by man. The purpose of this chapter has been to challenge preconceived ideas about church and encourage you to take a long, hard look at the questions of what church is and what some of the core elements of being church are.

The reality for many of us is that we have blindly followed popular thought on what church is and how it expresses itself. In doing this we may have missed out on the blessings that accompany church in its simplicity. My prayer is that we will begin to loose ourselves from our man-made bonds and enjoy God and each other in what Christ himself called his gathering. I hope this chapter causes you to seek God about what it means for you to be a part of his ecclesia.

y six years at St. Andrews was a wonderful season. I enjoyed my time both as a student and as a youth and university student worker. The biggest highlight of this experience—which came primarily through the student ministry that I led—was that I began to engage with the concept of every member ministry. By this I mean every member of the body of Christ having a role to play in the church. Let me share a bit about how all this came about.

Revolution

I had a wonderful friend who was passionate about church and about reaching people. He had come to university having had a lot of teaching about using cell groups as a means of reaching students. He was obsessed with this idea, and in the end he actually started up a student cell. (If you are not familiar with the cell model for student groups, visit www.fusion.uk.com.) These cell groups were led by students with some amount of supervision from a local church. Each cell had a facilitator who ran the meetings and kept everyone informed about what was going on in the weeks ahead. It was within this context that I had my first taste of every member ministry—or to put it in other words, the "priesthood of all believers." During the Reformation people developed the doctrine of every member ministry, and it's time we actually started practicing it. As some people say, orthodoxy must lead to orthopraxis—right doctrine must lead to right practice—or else we have fallen short.

My friend invited me to come on board as a supervisor for this group of people who had formed a cell. Initially there were just two groups, but at the end of two years we had around ten diverse cells in places ranging from student flats to a boarding school in the town. The cells were just the beginning; the next step was to have a celebration where all the cells could come together. I wanted to call these gatherings "cell-liberations," but my friends advised against it. Thank God for good friends.

Our cell groups were fruitful. Students were excited about being part of a group and being involved in an ongoing way. Each week someone would organize a fun icebreaker, someone else would share some revelation or teaching from God, and someone else would lead us in some form of worship. What was unique and inspiring about our little movement was that it was peer led, and it gave most people an opportunity to be involved and not just be spectators. My friend had a phrase for this kind of atmosphere; he called it a culture of contribution.

This experience of how exciting church can be has permanently ruined me and many of my friends: we can no longer go back to being pew warmers.

One Man Show

The New Testament church lived in a culture of contribution, where each person had something to offer. It saddens me when church meetings resemble a one-man show such as the *Late Show with David Letterman*. All these shows have a similar format: there's a band on the side to back up the host, but really the host is the main event. They tolerate guests on stage, but only because that keeps the viewing figures up and enhances the ratings. I don't believe this was Jesus' intention for his church. How is it that we now find ourselves in churches where 80 percent of the congregation are just spectators and almost all the rest are merely the supporting cast and technicians?

If we take Jesus as our ultimate example of a leader, we see that he did not operate as some kind of one-man show; instead, he encouraged his disciples to get involved. His goal was to teach them to minister rather than be the supporting act to the *Jesus Show*. Jesus had the kind of long-term thinking that many of us lack today. Because he knew he wouldn't be around forever, it was important for him to equip others to continue the work when he was gone rather than foster a dependence on him that would leave the disciples completely lost and ill-equipped for life after his departure.

The model of the CEO church leader is drawn from the secular world, not the Bible. In our world it is normal for one guy to be in charge and do all the work while the rest are just backup. I am not saying that this model of leadership is always wrong; it has its place. But the church is not the place for it, and to me the New Testament is very clear about that.

I have fallen into the trap of CEO-type leadership before. We all make the mistake of thinking that because we are the person best equipped to do a job, we should be the one to do it. This is a short-sighted approach. We forget that we were not always Bible teachers or group leaders. Whatever we do, we had to learn sometime—and pity the poor people we practiced on. Just as others did for us, we must release people to do certain tasks even if we think we could do a better job ourselves.

The frightening thing for me is that many people argue that the one-man band is the traditional and historic model of leadership the church has always used. In reality, this was something we adopted from pagans.

Pagan Origins

Some research has shown a considerable amount of pagan influence on the early church when Emperor Constantine came on the scene (see *The Open Church* by Jim Rutz and *Pagan Christianity* by Frank Viola and George Barna). Before his supposed conversion to Christianity, Constantine was a pagan through and through, and the pagan world he was used to worshiped in temples and had priests who supervised the worship. It was therefore natural for him to have Christian temples (i.e., churches) with priests (i.e., Christian leaders) running the show. For many pagans in the time of Constantine, the priest was a mystical person who had sole access to God and was in complete and utter control of the ceremony. It was to him that the divine mysteries had been revealed, and if anyone wanted to be in on the action, they had to go through him. When Constantine applied this model of worship to Christianity, we ended up with the clergy-versus-laity divide, which has plagued the church for hundreds of years. What we are experiencing today is the fruit of the adoption of a pagan model of worship.

This divide is something that the Cross addressed when the dividing veil was torn in two and we were all granted access to the Holy of Holies through the blood of Christ. It seems insane that we would abandon something that Christ has died for in favor of a pagan system of worship.

The Priesthood of All Believers

Many of you who are reading this book will be part of a church that finds its roots in the Reformation. It is easy to forget that one of the major points that Martin Luther fought for was the priesthood of all believers. How quickly we have returned to having priests, albeit in a slightly different guise. We may not call them priests, or Fathers—instead we call them pastors—but in many ways we still look to them as go-betweens for us in our relationship with God.

You may think I want to pick on pastors and label them as dominant people who want to have control over everything in our meetings. On the contrary, I am aware of many pastors who would quite happily have fewer duties, but their congregations put them on a pedestal as the person who can best connect with God on their behalf.

The idea of the priesthood of all believers was not an idea that Martin Luther conjured up out of nowhere. It was the practice of the early church. As we read about the early church from both New Testament and extrabiblical sources, we find that the modern idea of a pastor who runs everything was non-existent. In every house church there were elders who together shepherded the flock. And although there were leaders in the early church, such as James, Peter, and Paul, they were not dominant oppressors like many of those who existed in the time of

Luther. I am not saying that every leader who leads on his own is an oppressor, but any system that disempowers the majority to empower the minority is oppressive. If one man builds his ministry on the back of the children of God, this needs to be questioned.

We must remember that church *leadership* is different from having a *priest* who goes to God on your behalf. It is a tragedy that we have drifted back to the pagan models of leadership that Martin Luther fought to free the church from. The priesthood of all believers is something that should be central to our churches today.

Why Gather?

As I have mentioned, part of the reason why we tend toward this one-man leadership in our services is because we have grown accustomed to watching game shows and talk shows where one person hosts and orchestrates a few other participants, and the rest just sit there to be entertained.

I remember watching a clip on the BBC website about a massive US church who had just had their first service in a brand-new building. People were briefly interviewed as they came out of the meeting. One woman was asked how she found the service and her reply was, "It was a great production." She was right; after seeing clips of the service, I had to agree with her. However, I think she missed the point, or maybe it is our church gatherings that miss the point. Our meetings are not about entertainment and a great production.

A question I would like to raise is this: what is the point of a church service? Answering this question might help us work out what a church meeting should look like.

Many people may rush to say that the purpose of our church services is worship. There is some truth in that, but nothing in the New Testament suggests that we meet to worship. Romans 12 encourages us to live a lifestyle of worship every day as opposed to Sunday-to-Sunday worship expressed through the singing of hymns, etc. Another suggestion would be that we meet for teaching or discipleship, since that is the other major component of our modern church gatherings. Again, nothing in the New Testament suggests that this is the purpose of our meeting.

I have to admit that I struggled to answer this question until I read Frank Viola's book *Rethinking the Wineskin*. He argues convincingly that the purpose of Christian meetings according to the New Testament is encouragement for all. This might seem too simplistic for many of us, but we cannot afford to ignore this simple truth.

Let's look at two Scriptures:

What is it then, brothers? When you come together, each one of you has a psalm, has a teaching, has a revelation, has another language, has an interpretation. Let all things be done to build each other up. (1 Cor. 14:26)

Let us consider how to provoke one another to love and good works, not forsaking our own assembling together, as the custom of some is, but exhorting one another; and so much the more, as you see the Day approaching. (Heb. 10:24–25)

These Scriptures convey two things to me: first, that the purpose of the meeting is for mutual encouragement; and second, that we are all involved in achieving that goal.

Spirit-Led Meetings

One of the reasons we like to have someone in charge of the meeting is that we fear it may all go a bit weird if we give people freedom to share. What if the meeting is chaotic and ends up in a shambles? We need someone to keep things on track. This is true. We *should* have someone in charge of the meeting, and that person should be the Holy Spirit.

First Corinthians 12 shows us that the Holy Spirit is the one who gives people gifts.

> But to each one is given the manifestation of the Spirit for the profit of all. For to one is given through the Spirit the word of wisdom, and to another the word of knowledge, according to the same Spirit; to another faith, by the same Spirit; and to another gifts of healings, by the same Spirit; and to another workings of miracles; and to another prophecy; and to another discerning of spirits; to another different kinds of languages; and to another the interpretation of languages. But the one and the same Spirit works all of these, distributing to each one separately as he desires. (1 Cor. 12:7–11)

Two things to note in this passage are that the Holy Spirit gives to *all* and that he does so *as he pleases.*

It is not unreasonable to assume that whenever we come together, the Holy Spirit will direct the meeting and cause different people to make a contribution as he sees fit. In Acts 2 the Spirit gave the disciples the ability to speak in different languages. Do things have to be different now? And does the Spirit's enabling us apply only to speaking in tongues, or does it apply also to prophecy, songs, etc., as 1 Corinthians 14:26 suggests?

It occurred to me that because Paul spent so much time (in 1 Corinthians 12–14) explaining how things should be done decently and in order, things must *not* have been in order. Disorder in the Corinthian church may sound like a bad thing, but the reason for this was that everybody was *contributing*. They had a problem many of us wish our churches had: too many people wanted to participate in making church meetings happen. Anyone who has been in church leadership knows that this is not a problem we usually experience. In fact, it is often with great difficulty that we get people to take some kind of responsibility in the church. We must trust the Holy Spirit to lead our meetings as he gifts every member as he pleases.

Key Elements of Gatherings

It is hard to see how everyone can be involved in contributing to the meeting when we have church gatherings that are centered on preaching and singing songs. If a hundred people were preaching a sermon each week, we would be there all day. How many musicians can we have on our worship team? As many as we have inputs for in the mixing board? Even the best sound system could not manage much more than a hundred channels.

By exploring different ways of achieving our goal of mutual encouragement, we will find that it is possible to have many people involved in our meetings without the whole thing drifting into chaos. I would like to make some suggestions for what a meeting with a culture of contribution could possibly look like.

Jesus centered—breaking bread

The first way I suggest that we can mutually encourage one another is by the breaking of bread.

On the first day of the week, when the disciples were gathered together to break bread, Paul talked with them, intending to depart on the next day, and continued his speech until midnight. (Acts 20:7)

Even though this verse indicates that Paul preached a long sermon, the reason the disciples were gathered was for the breaking of bread. More verses can be added.

For first of all, when you come together in the assembly, I hear that divisions exist among you, and I partly believe it. For there also must be factions among you, that those who are approved may be revealed among you. When therefore you assemble yourselves together, it is not the Lord's supper that you eat. For in your eating each one takes his own supper first. One is hungry, and another is drunken. (1 Cor. 11:18–21)

Therefore, my brothers, when you come together to eat, wait one for another. (1 Cor. 11:33)

The context and wording of these scriptures suggest that breaking bread was the norm for these assemblies.

I have observed that many people underestimate the power of breaking bread. When people say it is symbolic, they also seem to assume that it is powerless—merely some procedure we should quickly perform and get over and done with. But if we agree that Christ should be central to our gatherings, then what better way to lift him up than to break bread together?

As I have read more and more of the Bible, I have realized that some symbolic acts carry with them spiritual realities. For example, in 1 Samuel 16:13 it says that Samuel performed the symbolic act of anointing David with oil. The end result was a very real encounter with the Holy Spirit who came upon him from that day on. Clearly the anointing with oil was not empty symbolism. In the same way, I do not believe that Communion is empty symbolism. If it were, people would not experience weakness, sickness, and death as a result of taking Communion unworthily (see 1 Cor. 11:27–30).

Breaking bread is an incredible act of worship that puts Christ in his rightful place above all things. When we break bread, we acknowledge the creator God who was willing to come and die for us; we retell the greatest story ever, in which the God of heaven and earth came down and lived among us, suffered a horrible death for humankind, and was raised up to sit at the right hand of God.

As I write this, it is only a few days away from Christmas and I have Christmas carols playing in the background. It is hard to hold back tears as I consider afresh how important Christmas is in the incredible story of God's work. This brings me to a place of worship, awe, and wonder at the fact that God would do such a thing—that he would come down and dwell bodily among us. When we celebrate the Lord's Supper, we have the opportunity to experience the glory of Christmas in a unique way.

The breaking of bread is the greatest act of worship we can ever engage in, and it is the foundation of all the other parts of our meetings that can encourage us.

Reality check—confession

Because breaking bread is so important, Paul encourages a little preparation before we dive in. We are invited to make sure that when we take Communion we do not do so in an unworthy

up

manner. "But let a man examine himself, and so let him eat of the bread, and drink of the cup" (1 Cor. 11:28). This self-examination will lead us to a place of confession. We can ask the Holy Spirit to show us anything in our lives that we need to confess, and as we do this we have an opportunity to confess to the Lord and to each other.

DOWN

In Matthew, Christ tells us that when we come to bring an offering to God, we must make sure that there is no person with whom we are not at peace. Otherwise we should stop there, go and make our peace with our brother, and then come back. "If therefore you are offering your gift at the altar, and there remember that your brother has anything against you, leave your gift there before the altar, and go your way. First be reconciled to your brother, and then come and offer your gift" (Matt. 5:23–24). If we have wronged someone and are convicted in our heart, we have an opportunity to confess our sin against our brother. On the other hand, if our brother seeks our forgiveness and we withhold it, our hardheartedness is exposed. Either way, through our self-examination and through his Spirit, God can bring conviction and cleansing.

IN

What better encouragement can there be than restored relationships with one another and a restored relationship with God when sin has been in the way? "Confess your offenses to one another, and pray for one another, that you may be healed. The insistent prayer of a righteous person is powerfully effective" (James 5:16). Isn't it amazing to think that out of the simple process of examining ourselves before Communion, we have the opportunity to confess to one another, pray for one another, and find healing?

OUT

Prayer is the next natural step in taking Communion.

Fresh encounter—prayer

In an earlier chapter I mentioned that prayer was simply communication with God. We can pray for ourselves or, as mentioned above, for each other. It is natural for us to engage in prayer when we come together, since many of us come with things on our hearts that we need to share with God and each other.

How many times have we come to a meeting with many things on our mind and been told simply to forget about them, which is something we find nearly impossible to do? What may be more effective is for one or two people to stand with us in bringing these things before the Lord.

When we come to take part in Communion, we come not only to remember what Christ has done for us as an exclusively mental exercise but also to appropriate afresh the power of the Cross in our lives. The work of the Cross brought physical, spiritual, and emotional restoration. As we take Communion, we ought to pray for each other that we may receive God's healing in every one of these areas of our lives. Prayer can take many forms as the Spirit of Christ leads us. As we confess sin and pray with and for one another, we receive forgiveness afresh, we receive cleansing afresh, and we receive healing afresh.

Spontaneity—praise and thanksgiving

A key part of breaking bread is praise and thanksgiving. As we come together and think about what Christ has done for us, we cannot help but offer thanksgiving to him. Many times when I have taken Communion and experienced the power of God, I have felt incredible excitement and have had the desire to burst into song.

My vivid imagination pictures an early church meeting where people are so excited about God that they spontaneously burst

UP

DOWN

IN

OUT

into songs of praise and worship. I have read that such spontaneity is common in revivals. Someone will burst into a song inspired by the Holy Spirit, and everyone else will sing along until the Holy Spirit moves them onto something else. Throughout the history of the church, thanksgiving and praise have been a natural part of honoring Christ.

Loving one another—fellowship

Another much-overlooked aspect of breaking bread is fellowship. I was blissfully unaware of this until several years ago when I discovered the expression "love feast" in my Bible and some other literature. I became rather curious. For me the phrase "love feast" did not initially conjure up the kinds of images you would associate with church, so I had to dig deeper. I discovered that what we call Communion today is a miniaturized version of what the New Testament church engaged in, and also that we put a greater emphasis on the symbolic aspect of the meal.

Before I move on to explain the love feast, I must draw your attention to the fact that for the early disciples the expression "breaking bread" was not a religious one. It simply meant that people shared a meal together. So when we read in Acts 2 about the disciples breaking bread in each other's homes, this is not saying that they had Communion like we have Communion. It means they had meals together. I suspect that the way we have Communion today has evolved as a result of an emphasis on liturgy and probably even has a little to do with convenience. I grew up in an Anglican Church where we had the wafer and wine. Many people would find it much more convenient to have the wafer and wine than to prepare and consume a whole meal. However, because none of us wants to miss out on the mystery and power of liturgy, we still want to engage in the Lord's Supper. So today in many churches, instead of a full meal we have a section of the service where we can share Communion. For many of us, the love feast is a thing of the past.

A love feast was a gathering of the saints where they had a meal together in something of a party atmosphere and then shared Communion as part of that feast. Communion didn't involve a little cup and small piece of bread. It was part of a full meal, which is why Paul had to rebuke people for drinking too much at the love feast. To me this seems like a party (see 1 Cor. 11:20–22). And the observance of the Lord's Supper was the peak of this party.

Many churches have managed to reduce fellowship to a cup of tea and a biscuit at the end of our meeting. It seems we have much more important things to do than spend time fellowshiping with one another. Obviously our church meetings are not the only place we can fellowship together, but the New Testament Christians took this aspect of church life very seriously, so much so that it is one of the things mentioned in Acts as a pursuit to which the church devoted themselves: "They continued steadfastly in the apostles' teaching and fellowship, in the breaking of bread, and prayer" (Acts 2:42).

Considering that Christ said people would know that we follow him by the way we love one another (John 13:35), does it not make sense to commit to spending time together and building relationships?

When I first discovered the love feast, I encouraged my university Christian Union to try it. We had several love feasts where we spent time enjoying one another instead of rushing in and out of the meeting. I know for a fact that the strength of a church is not measured by the preaching, the worship band, or the ministry programs. It is measured by the love people have for one another, and that only comes through genuine fellowship.

Open space—Bible and prophecy

UP

As we seek to put Christ first in our gatherings, we must make space for him to speak to us. Many times when we have Communion, not only do we sense God's closeness, but we sense that he is close enough to speak to us. God may speak to us personally, affirming that we have received forgiveness of sins, or he may speak to us corporately.

DOWN

I believe that a loving God who is given room to be Lord in our meeting will always have something to say to us that will encourage us. Even if this is a word of rebuke, in the long run, if we confess, pray, and receive God's healing, it will bring us to a place of encouragement.

I believe there are other ways that God speaks to us in our gatherings. For example, he speaks through the reading of the Scriptures as the Holy Spirit prompts us to seek out a passage. He also speaks through prophetic utterances, which Paul tells us to be aware of in Corinthians: "Let the prophets speak, two or three, and let the others discern. But if a revelation is made to another sitting by, let the first keep silent. For you all can prophesy one by one, that all may learn, and all may be exhorted" (1 Cor. 14:29–30). Note here that Paul says we can all prophesy so that we all may be encouraged.

IN

OUT

I know many of us feel that the best way to hear from God in our meetings is through a prepared sermon. Preaching has its place in the body of Christ; but if we give it an exclusive place, we have yet to experience the wonders of giving God the freedom to speak to his people in a variety of ways. Many of us have been in meetings when the Holy Spirit has moved someone to share a powerful word with the rest of the congregation. Maybe it was a scripture or some prophetic utterance that fit the church's specific circumstances. Many of us have come to believe that such moments are few and far between, but I believe we can come to the place where we experience such moments on a regular basis.

My Present Experience

What I have suggested for gatherings in a culture of contribution may seem like a distant reality: a church meeting where people can share what God is speaking to them and not rely primarily on a sermon. It is possible, but it takes time. I presently find myself in a church that is journeying toward the kind of meetings we can now only dream of. We are not there yet by a long shot, but we have traveled a good way away from the kind of service that is dominated by a handful of people to the kind of meeting that leaves room for everyone to participate. Being in this church has given me a lot of hope about what I believe God is sowing in my heart regarding church meetings. This is not an unreachable dream, even though it could take quite a long time to achieve.

In this chapter I have taken us on a long journey. I have suggested that our present model of running our meetings may fall short of the goal that God expresses in Scripture. Many churches are presently so dependent on human conductors of our meetings that we are scared to release the meeting into the hands of God so that every person can make a contribution to the meeting through his promptings. I have also suggested that we may have missed the purpose of our meetings and therefore may have lost sight of how to run and structure our meetings.

I would not dare to suggest that I have all the answers. In reality I probably have more questions than answers, but I do not find that the least bit intimidating. It's actually freeing.

Because of the questions I've been willing to ask, I have made discoveries that have brought me into a deeper relationship with God. And because I still have many unanswered questions, I have not dared to present a definitive list of "seven ways to run a meeting" or "six ways to have a spontaneous service." That's not my style anyway. My goal is simply to get people to think outside the box and ask God questions that may challenge some of their previous ways of thinking.

God has, however, given me insights into some questions. I believe in the priesthood of all believers. I believe in a church where 100 percent of the people participate. I believe in a church where Christ is at the center and is given the freedom to do what he wants when we gather together in his name. I believe that the blood shed during the revolutionary Reformation was not in vain but was to set the masses free to encounter God in a new and personal way. I believe we have the opportunity to make a fresh push into the unknown, as many who have gone before have done.

Let us have enough faith to trust not only that God's way is the best way but also that if we let God run his gatherings, they will not descend into chaos.

10. True Shepherds

What does it means to be a leader? This is a big question we face in the church today.

Some of the different answers to this question are based on cultural experiences and personal experiences. Being a Sierra Leonean, some of my past views of leadership were dictatorial. In Sierra Leone my observation was that being a leader meant you could do what you want. Our nation has a long history of political leaders who were (and some of them still are) only out for themselves. Once they come into power, their goal is to line their pockets as much as they can before they lose their position. They are not there to serve at all; on the contrary, they want to be treated as kings waited upon hand and foot. Their understanding of servant leadership is, "I lead. You serve."

Thankfully God has opened my eyes to some leadership principles that have helped shape me and transform my mind. The more my mind has been transformed, the more I have been grieved by what I sometimes see in the church. It seems like some Christian leaders have learned about leadership from the same school as some of the political leaders of Sierra Leone's past.

I have read of ministries where even though they operate under charitable status, a vast amount of their income goes toward their own personal charitable fund called *self*. Leaders of some of these ministries spend millions on private jets and hotel suites from money given as a "widow's mite" (Mark 12:38–44 tells the story of the widow's mite). I fail to see what connection these self-serving, megalomaniac leaders have with Jesus.

No doubt God uses many of these people, because he is much more gracious than I am, but that does not mean he approves of their lifestyle. Many times we think that any blessing or fruitfulness we experience in ministry is a sign of God's approval. We fail to recognize how gracious God is toward humanity. I know from experience that you can be doing the wrong thing and still experience God's blessings in a ministry, because he is a gracious God.

What does God think when he sees some of our Christian leaders today? Can you imagine Jesus flying around in a private jet paid for by the offerings from the poor (which were supposed to go back to the poor)? Can you imagine Jesus being followed around by an entourage of bodyguards like a celebrity? The only guards he was familiar with were the ones who led him to his death.

We need to look anew at leadership and learn as much as we can from the Bible rather than from our society.

Jesus on Leadership

Jesus gave some clear guidance on what leaders are supposed to be like and not be like.

But Jesus summoned them, and said, "You know that the rulers of the nations lord it over them, and their great ones exercise authority over them. It shall not be so among you, but whoever desires to become great among you shall be your servant. Whoever desires to be first among you shall be your bondservant, even as the Son of Man came not to be served, but to serve, and to give his life as a ransom for many." (Matt. 20:25–28)

The call to be a leader is a call to become a servant. Not just any servant, but a slave, because that is what the word *bondservant* means. This is the heart of New Testament leadership as described by Jesus himself, and he lived this in an exemplary manner.

In the parallel passage in Luke, Jesus speaks specifically about being the ones who serve at the table rather than the ones who sit at the table.

He said to them, "The kings of the nations lord it over them, and those who have authority over them are called 'benefactors.' But not so with you. But one who is the greater among you, let him become as the younger, and one who is governing, as one who serves. For who is greater, one who sits at the table, or one who serves? Isn't it he who sits at the table? But I am in the midst of you as one who serves. But you are those who have continued with me in my trials. I confer on you a kingdom, even as my Father conferred on me, that you may eat and drink at my table in my Kingdom. You will sit on thrones, judging the twelve tribes of Israel." (Luke 22:25–30)

UP

DOWN

IN

OUT

Jesus then tells Peter to establish his brothers: "You, when once you have turned again, establish your brothers" (22:32).

As servants our job is to help others become established in faith and not simply to establish ourselves. Many times as leaders we are tempted to use people for our own ends, to help establish a personal ministry or help us take the next career step.

After Peter's denial, Jesus wanted to give Peter a fresh commission. He focused not on Peter and his ministry but on the fact that he wanted Peter to serve the church by taking care of his sheep and feeding his lambs.

> So when they had eaten their breakfast, Jesus said to Simon Peter, "Simon, son of Jonah, do you love me more than these?" He said to him, "Yes, Lord; you know that I have affection for you." He said to him, "Feed my lambs." He said to him again a second time, "Simon, son of Jonah, do you love me?" He said to him, "Yes, Lord; you know that I have affection for you." He said to him, "Tend my sheep." He said to him the third time, "Simon, son of Jonah, do you have affection for me?" Peter was grieved because he asked him the third time, "Do you have affection for me?" He said to him, "Lord, you know everything. You know that I have affection for you." Jesus said to him, "Feed my sheep." (John 21:15–17)

I don't think it would be going too far to make a connection between Jesus' statement about waiting on tables in Luke and the feeding of the lambs here in John. Jesus is basically inviting Peter to serve the church, to become as one who waits on tables. This was his call to church leadership.

The Example of Christ as a Leader

Christ's commands for leaders were not empty words but were displayed in his ministry on earth. Christ lived out what he commanded. Even though he was and is the King of kings and had every right to lord it over us because he is the Lord of lords, he chose to come and live as a servant.

> Have this in your mind, which was also in Christ Jesus, who, existing in the form of God, didn't consider equality with God a thing to be grasped, but emptied himself, taking the form of a servant, being made in the likeness of men. And being found in human form, he humbled himself, becoming obedient to death, yes, the death of the cross. (Phil. 2:5–8)

Jesus was explicit about his own purpose, which was to be a servant to men—to the point that he sacrificed himself on the Cross. "Whoever desires to be first among you shall be your bondservant, even as the Son of Man came not to be served, but to serve, and to give his life as a ransom for many" (Matt. 20:27–28).

Ezekiel's Warning to Shepherds

One of the reasons the church sometimes has the problem of poor leadership is that we have ignored some of the guiding principles in the Bible for what we should expect from leaders. In Ezekiel chapter 34, there is a declaration of God's judgment on the shepherds of Israel who did not lead as they should. God condemned these leaders for doing the following:

1. *Feeding off the sheep instead of feeding the sheep.* One thing that really breaks my heart is when I see church leaders use people

rather than empower people. Often I find that people are used merely as a source of income for the church, or they are seen as laborers serving the egoistic and self-centered visions of church leaders rather than as colaborers with Christ. According to Ephesians 4:11–12, the role of church leaders is to equip the saints for works of service; they are supposed to empower people. When a church leader's relationship with the congregation has become primarily about what he or she can get instead of what he or she can give, then that leader has truly missed the point.

2. *Not strengthening the diseased, healing the sick, or binding up the broken.* Another role of the leader is to help people overcome obstacles in their life, especially those of a spiritual nature. It is of infinite value to have someone come alongside and help us walk through what might feel like the valley of the shadow of death. I am not saying that leaders have to be the personal answer to everyone's problem; what I am saying is that they can play a major role in helping people work through struggles. For example, James says that if anyone is sick, let him call on the elders to lay hands on him and pray for him (James 5:14). I am struck by the number of people facing emotional challenges who need some kind of support or counseling. This is the kind of help that leaders can often give that will only cost them time. For leaders to neglect these areas of ministry certainly grieves God.

3. *Not bringing back those driven away.* God invites church leaders in the body of Christ to seek out those who have had a difficulty with church and see them restored to the body. What I find instead is that people are driven away by church leaders rather than sought out and brought back. Many times leaders display judgmental attitudes rather than true love and acceptance. Much of what passes as the "defense of the truth" is actually just good

old-fashioned Pharisaic religion. People who do not fit neatly and perfectly into our religious boxes are ostracized. It is almost understandable if sheep bite each other and drive each other away, but when Christian leaders initiate and model such behavior, I believe God's heart is seriously grieved.

A friend highlighted the fact that the phrase "not bringing back those driven away" could also be applied to the role of leaders in seeking out the marginalized of our society. Often those who are on the fringes of a society are ignored at best or persecuted at worst. If the body of Christ does not make room for them in society, who will? Leaders can take the lead in this kind of ministry.

4. *Not seeking that which was lost.* Another significant challenge we face as the church is to shift away from being self-focused, self-sustaining, bless-me clubs to being outward-looking, community-reaching followers of Christ. As a leader, I know how much easier it is to do in-house ministry, but I am constantly challenged to encourage others and model to them how to look beyond ourselves into the world around that desperately needs Jesus and all he has to offer.

5. *Having ruled with force.* Finally I would like to comment on leaders who rule with force. Leading by force completely contradicts being a shepherd. A shepherd is one who cares for and nurtures his sheep. The model of leadership we see in Christ is to engage people with compassion and gentleness.

As I understand it, Christ is the over-shepherd and leaders of the church are under-shepherds. If Christ does not use force, what gives us the right to use force when we lead others? I have heard there are two ways of leading sheep: you can drive and beat them from behind to get them to go where you want, or you can walk in front of them and they will follow you. A true shepherd cultivates a relationship with his sheep and does not have to drive them from behind.

Paul's Requirements

We have explored poor leadership in an Old Testament passage. Now I would like to turn to the New Testament, specifically 1 Timothy and Titus, and look at Paul's description of a good leader and the requirements for those who desire to become leaders. Paul focuses not only on abilities but also on character. Reading these passages, you get a clear sense that there is a standard that leaders need to attain to.

> This is a faithful saying: if a man seeks the office of an overseer, he desires a good work. The overseer therefore must be without reproach, the husband of one wife, temperate, sensible, modest, hospitable, good at teaching; not a drinker, not violent, not greedy for money, but gentle, not quarrelsome, not covetous; one who rules his own house well, having children in subjection with all reverence; (but if a man doesn't know how to rule his own house, how will he take care of the assembly of God?) not a new convert, lest being puffed up he fall into the same condemnation as the devil. Moreover he must have good testimony from those who are outside, to avoid falling into reproach and the snare of the devil. Servants [or deacons], in the same way, must be reverent, not double-tongued, not addicted to much wine, not greedy for money; holding the mystery of the faith in a pure conscience. Let them also first be tested; then let them serve if they are blameless. Their wives in the same way must be reverent, not slanderers, temperate, faithful in all things. Let

servants be husbands of one wife, ruling their children and their own houses well. For those who have served well gain for themselves a good standing, and great boldness in the faith which is in Christ Jesus. (1 Tim. 3:1–13)

I left you in Crete for this reason, that you would set in order the things that were lacking, and appoint elders in every city, as I directed you; if anyone is blameless, the husband of one wife, having children who believe, who are not accused of loose or unruly behavior. For the overseer must be blameless, as God's steward; not self-pleasing, not easily angered, not given to wine, not violent, not greedy for dishonest gain; but given to hospitality, a lover of good, sober minded, fair, holy, self-controlled; holding to the faithful word which is according to the teaching, that he may be able to exhort in the sound doctrine, and to convict those who contradict him. For there are also many unruly men, vain talkers and deceivers, especially those of the circumcision, whose mouths must be stopped; men who overthrow whole houses, teaching things which they ought not, for dishonest gain's sake. (Titus 1:5–11)

It is at our own peril that we ignore these requirements for biblical leadership that are so clearly laid out. Many of us will recognize that these standards are very high and that if we actually applied them, we might struggle to find the leaders we need to continue our churches and ministries. Our real need for leaders is not, however, a good enough reason for ignoring the high standards that God has deliberately set in place. The unfortunate truth is that many times what we are looking for in leaders is charisma, talents, and spiritual gifts above anything else. So people who have great communication skills and could success-fully work as salesmen or motivational speakers can decide they are preachers, and we will all come and listen; and before you know it, they have thriving churches, not based on their char-acter or calling but simply on their ability to entertain a crowd using the Scriptures.

Because of this kind of scenario, we find erroneous teach-ings occasionally rising up in the body of Christ. If, for example, we do not heed the warning the Bible gives about not having leaders who are lovers of money, we will end up with preachers who preach messages that are almost entirely focused on money and how God wants to make us rich. We then end up with mate-rialistic disciples whose goal in life is to make money and be comfortable rather than bring glory to Christ. Having money as a primary focus prevents them from fulfilling their true calling, which could well require them not to have a lot of money and to suffer.

Team Leadership

An exciting discovery I made in the Bible is the role of team. From Moses to Paul, the Bible shows us multiple expressions of this shared kind of leadership.

In Exodus, Moses's father-in-law, Jethro, teaches him about delegation and sharing the workload (Exod. 18:13–26). In this model of team leadership, we understand that many times the burden of leading a group of people can simply be too much for one person. No one can successfully bear the burden of leading a large number of people by himself or herself. The burden of leading the people of Israel was spread over many, and only when one of the leaders could not handle a situation would Moses be brought in to judge.

The New Testament also provides examples of team leadership. In Acts 15 we see that when a major decision needed to be made, the apostles and elders discussed it and made a prayerful decision about the matters at hand.

> Some men came down from Judea and taught the brothers, "Unless you are circumcised after the custom of Moses, you can't be saved." Therefore when Paul and Barnabas had no small discord and discussion with them, they appointed Paul and Barnabas, and some others of them, to go up to Jerusalem to the apostles and elders about this question. (Acts 15:1–2)

A second reason for having leadership teams is that wiser decisions can be made, because no one person has all the wisdom required for every situation. Proverbs puts it very strongly: "Where there is no wise guidance, the nation falls, but in the multitude of counselors there is victory" (Prov. 11:14).

The final reason I want to give for my strong belief in team leadership is this: there is a necessity for diversity in order to meet the varied needs of a group of people and meet the requirements that God has for his church. First Corinthians 12 explains that the people of God can be likened to a body that is made up of many parts, each performing its function as enabled by the Holy Spirit. So in any given situation, it is wise to have a diverse set of leaders, each with different strengths and gifts to contribute.

It then makes perfect sense to me that Paul, in Ephesians 4, states that bringing the church to maturity requires not one person but five (or four, depending on whom you ask) who are gifted and empowered by God and are themselves a gift from God to his people.

He gave some to be apostles; and some, prophets; and some, evangelists; and some, shepherds and teachers; for the perfecting of the saints, to the work of serving, to the building up of the body of Christ; until we all attain to the unity of the faith, and of the knowledge of the Son of God, to a full grown man, to the measure of the stature of the fullness of Christ; that we may no longer be children, tossed back and forth and carried about with every wind of doctrine, by the trickery of men, in craftiness, after the wiles of error; but speaking truth in love, we may grow up in all things into him, who is the head, Christ; from whom all the body, being fitted and knit together through that which every joint supplies, according to the working in measure of each individual part, makes the body increase to the building up of itself in love. (Eph. 4:11–16)

It is sad that in the history of the church we have ignored the very gifts that Christ has given to bring his church to maturity. In the fivefold ministry described in the passage above, each person brings a unique flavor of Christ into the body of Christ. It excites me that more and more churches today are recognizing the importance of team leadership and are asking the Holy Spirit to release apostles, prophets, pastors, teachers, and evangelists within their congregations.

Fivefold Ministry

The subject of the fivefold ministry is not an easy one to address. There are many opinions of what the five ministers' roles entail. I wish I could say that I was about to give you a definitive explanation of the fivefold ministry, but sadly I am just going to add to the myriad of opinions out there. I, like everyone else, have taken time to read the Scriptures and meditate on them, asking God for insight and revelation, so it's up to you to discern the validity of my approach.

The first thing to point out about these ministries is that they exist to equip others for service. Many times people make the mistake of thinking that the five poor ministers are supposed to accomplish the entire ministry themselves, which results in overworked pastors who face burnout. Paul, however, says these ministers are to equip the rest of the body to minister. With this in mind, I see the prophet not simply as someone who brings the prophetic word of the Lord but also as one who teaches and helps others to prophesy, especially those whom God may be calling to some kind of prophetic ministry. This same principle applies to the other four types of ministers, too: they are called to exercise their gift and also to equip others to minister in that area. So now let's look at the five ministries.

Apostles

The New Testament describes apostles and prophets as the foundation of God's household (Eph. 2:19–22). By using the apostle Paul as an example of apostleship, we discover some fresh insights into what an apostle is and the ministry apostles perform. From the Greek, an apostle is a "sent-out one," or a messenger. From my understanding of the Scriptures, an apostle is one sent out with the authority of Jesus Christ (see Gal. 1:1). Apostles have authority to preach and teach (1 Tim. 2:7; 2 Tim. 1:11). They have authority to speak on God's behalf (2 Pet. 3:2; Eph. 3:5). They have authority to establish and strengthen churches (1 Cor. 3:6). They also have God-given authority to be involved in church leadership and other strategic leadership spheres. I believe we find apostles leading large corporations or organizations or sometimes even countries. Lastly, apostles have an authority for the display of signs and wonders (2 Cor. 12:2; Acts 2:43).

Prophets

Prophets, as the name implies, are those involved in prophesying, which from the Greek implies those who "foretell." Although it is true that God sometimes reveals the future to prophets, we see from the Old Testament that being a prophet is very much about revealing God's heart in the present. Old Testament prophets spoke on behalf of God, sometimes seeing into the future and sometimes discerning the hearts of men and God and warning of God's wrath. Ultimately they provoked God's people into a deeper relationship with God when they were at risk of faltering or wandering away, or when they already had. Any Christian can hear from God and prophesy, but a higher level of authority is bestowed on a prophet, allowing him or her to prophesy over people or churches or even cities, nations, and national or international leaders.

Evangelists

Evangelists are those whom God has gifted with an ability to bring the good news to others. Although we are *all* called to make disciples, God has gifted some people with an incredible ability to explain the good news in such a way that people are drawn to Christ.

Pastors

Pastors or shepherds are those whom God has equipped with an ability to care for people and provide leadership in a way that guides others on their journey toward him. Pastors have a God-given capacity to show compassion to others. They desire to help people work through difficult aspects of the Christian life. They will search out the weak and the struggling among us.

Teachers

Teachers are those whom God has equipped to help people learn truth that will change their lives. I believe one of the great gifts of teachers is the ability to come alongside people to help them grow into Christlikeness. In the New Testament a teacher was not just a lecturer but was a master discipler, one whom privileged disciples would spend time with to learn as much as they could from their teacher. Teachers were to be people that the students could imitate. That's why it isn't weird for Paul to say, "Imitate me, just as I imitate Christ" (1 Cor. 11:1 NLT). Paul's audience would have understood him perfectly, especially if they were Jewish and were used to the idea of followers of rabbis imitating the rabbi.

As we look at people in the New Testament such as Paul, Agabus, and Philip who had ministries we could define as one of the fivefold, we see that their ministries were not limited to one place or one group of believers. Paul's apostolic gospel preaching was not limited to one location (Rom. 15:19); Agabus was a prophet who came down from Judea to warn Paul (Acts 21:10); and Philip was an evangelist who traveled to Samaria to preach (Acts 8:5). These men show the importance of translocal ministries, but a church group also needs some permanent and resident leaders in their midst. This is where local elders come in.

Local Elders

Local elders are yet another kind of leadership team in the New Testament. These people must have been important because, as mentioned earlier, Paul gives detailed guidelines regarding who is suitable for this role.

Two Greek words are translated as "elder" in the New Testament: *presbuteros* (where we get *presbyter* from) and *episkopos* (where we get *episcopal* from). *Presbuteros* can be translated as literally an "elder person," and *episkopos* can be translated as "bishop" or "overseer." Putting these definitions together, "elder" is the title given to the person and overseeing is the job that he or she does.

Coming up with a hard and fast view of how elders should operate today is difficult since the New Testament environment was different from what we are used to today. Back then, people met in homes rather than in large congregations, and when people referred to a church, they could be talking about a group in a city. Hence, Paul talked about appointing elders in each city (Titus 1:5). The idea of the city church or the house church is less common today.

Early Christians also would have been more familiar with the idea of elders because elders were a part of Jewish culture. All the way back to Genesis and through to Revelation, there are references to the role of elders in Jewish society. Particularly notable are the seventy elders appointed to help Moses lead Israel (Num. 11:16–26).

We see in the Scriptures that elders were involved in the day-to-day operations of the church. They taught (1 Tim. 3:2), oversaw (Acts 20:28), gave counsel (Acts 21:23–25), prayed for the sick (James 5:14), and imparted spiritual gifts (1 Tim. 4:14).

Elders were supported by deacons, which virtually means servants. One way of looking at the difference between an elder and a deacon is highlighted by the twelve apostles' appointment of Stephen and others to serve the poor (see Acts 6:1–6). The twelve wanted to focus on the spiritual side of the work, such as prayer and the preaching of the word, but they did not want the necessary, practical side of the work—such as feeding people—to be neglected. The deacons were selected to be in charge of practical tasks.

Again we see a model of team leadership: the early church team consisted of those called to serve by leading in prayer and the word and those called to lead by serving the poor and the needy.

Training Leaders

One of the big questions we face today is about how leaders are appointed and trained. The most recurrent answer from Scripture—one which cannot be overstated—is that the Holy Spirit appoints leaders. And it seems that existing leaders recognize potential leaders and train them to be leaders. For example, in Acts 13 the Holy Spirit spoke to the church to separate Paul and Barnabas for ministry; the elders then laid hands on them and sent them out.

Many leaders can identity those who are potential leaders. In fact, most Christians can see leadership abilities in people, which is why Peter invited the Christians to choose seven men who could serve within the body. "Therefore select from among you, brothers, seven men of good report, full of the Holy Spirit and of wisdom, whom we may appoint over this business" (Acts 6:3).

We also learn from Scripture that some people recognize leadership abilities in people before others do. Barnabas, for example, saw Paul's potential quite early on, when no one really trusted Paul because of his past (Acts 9:26–27).

In regard to training, I think we need to regain the lost art of training leaders through a mentoring relationship. This was the kind of relationship that Paul had with Timothy, where he modeled good leadership to him and encouraged him in leadership. Today we prefer to send people to lectures at university or some other training program and give them a sheet of paper saying they are now qualified to minister. We don't have to look far to find a different way to train leaders. Our ultimate example is Jesus, who shared much of his life with his disciples and taught them many things by his example in a hands-on way. This form of training was and always will be the tougher road to follow since it is more costly to the trainer. But if we take leadership within the body of Christ as seriously as Jesus did, we'll view this as a small price to pay.

God wants there to be leaders among his people. How leadership is done and what leaders look like is set out in the Scriptures, and we ignore this teaching at our own peril. My prayer is that in the season ahead we will have leaders who are full of integrity and whose passion is to care for those in their charge; who are not burned out from stress because they have too much work to do on their own; who are part of a team that is diverse enough to meet the many needs of the body. I pray we would openly talk about apostles and prophets and see them rise up in many places. I pray that many leaders would make it a priority and invest adequate time to train up the next generation of leaders.

If my prayers are answered, and I believe they will be, the church that Christ will come back to will look very different from the church we are part of today.

UP

DOWN

IN

OUT

Section D

Look OUT to the world

11. The Spheres of Society

Several years ago I was at a conference on evangelism in Stirling. One seminar I attended had the specific aim of helping Christians in the secular workplace. I don't really know what I was doing there, because the longest I have ever been in a workplace outside Christian ministry is three or four months of summer work while I was a student. I guess I went out of curiosity, and I was changed.

The session speaker, Mark Greene from the London Institute of Contemporary Christianity, showed me areas of my thought that were misguided. He helped me to see that based on the number of Christians in the workplace and the amount of time they spend there, we need to do more to equip those people to minister within that context.

A secret, unspoken hierarchy exists in the Christian world and is perpetuated by both those in "full-time Christian ministry" and those who are in "secular jobs." I use these labels simply to communicate quickly and succinctly what I am getting at.

Many Christians think that "full-time ministry," such as being a pastor or missionary, is the highest form of work that someone can engage in, and that any other work is second best.

I once heard someone humorously describe the hierarchy like this: at the top of the ladder are pastors and other Christian workers; next are those in the caring professions, because they are helping people; next are teachers, whom we respect for the work they do with our kids; then come business people, whom we merely tolerate because they can finance church projects with big offerings; and at the bottom of the pile, by default, are politicians and lawyers.

Mark Greene gave an example that cut to the heart. During a church service a teacher by profession decided to volunteer to help with Sunday school and was hauled up to the front for prayer. The teacher realized that he had never before received prayer in the service, even though he had taught in schools for many years; but now all of a sudden when he was "ministering" in church, he was brought to the front for special recognition. The man realized that the church's Sunday school ministry was being valued above his lifelong ministry of teaching.

This encounter with Mark Greene led me to repent of some arrogant, self-righteous, and judgmental views I had held up to that point. The encounter also got me thinking more and more about the workplace and about how important it is for me as a Christian worker always to be thinking about how I can equip the people I work with for their ministry in the workplace. Once this groundwork had been laid, I was ready to receive some further insight into this area.

Old Testament Template

The next step for me was discovering the teaching by Landa Cope on what she calls the "Old Testament template" (see Further Reading section). Her way of looking at missions and the command to go and make disciples has been significant in shaping my approach to ministry. Instead of trying to summarize the teaching, though, I will describe how it impacted me.

I, like many other Christians, had made the mistake of dividing the world into sacred and secular categories, which had led me to the idea that "full-time" Christian work was more significant than "secular" work. The artificial dichotomy between sacred and secular work did not find its origins in early Christianity; in fact, many streams of Christianity throughout history, including the Celtic saints of the sixth and seventh centuries, have rejected any such divisions. This better way of looking at the world acknowledges that we are all called and equipped by God to serve in the one world that has many spheres, each of them different, but valuable in the eyes of God.

The sacred-secular divide has forced many Christians into a very weird form of evangelism and discipleship. Our evangelism is often focused on leading people to a salvation experience, and our discipleship trains them simply to be religious people. I believe that God is calling us to something far greater, and to be honest, far more difficult. We are to disciple not only individuals but also entire communities of which individuals are a part.

Landa Cope points out that discipling entire communities of heathen nations is nothing new to God. God took the people of Israel from being a random bunch of beaten down nomads to being a powerful nation still respected today. God gave Moses the keys to be able to disciple a nation from "zero to hero." Looking through the books of Moses with these new glasses, we discover that for thousands of years God has been discipling nations and providing guiding principles for every area of life, not just religious life.

People have identified seven or eight spheres of society, depending on how they organize them. I will go with the following eight:

- Government and politics
- Business and economics
- Family and community
- Arts, entertainment, and sports
- Health, science, and technology
- Education
- Media
- Religion and spirituality

If you read through the Old Testament, you will find that God has something to say about every one of these areas. Since God is into reality, he naturally wants to equip us for the realities of life. For example, did you know that the command not to circumcise before the eighth day is not just for religious reasons but is for practical medical reasons? Vitamin K, which is essential for blood clotting, is not usually produced till day eight of a newborn's life. Circumcising any earlier would result in the child's bleeding to death. Another example is how God used Moses' father-in-law, Jethro, to help Moses organize a system for governing the people in which every tribe was represented. Does that sound familiar? It could be where we first got the idea of proportional representation in government. These examples show that some of God's interventions were not only for religious reasons but for the health of society and even in some cases for saving the life of a child. God is indeed a good and practical God.

Go into All the Cosmos

Because we live in a world with distinct spheres of society, it makes sense that God would want us to be equipped to impact and disciple the spheres in the way that he intended them to be.

> He said to them, "Go into all the world, and preach the Good News to the whole creation. He who believes and is baptized will be saved; but he who disbelieves will be condemned. These signs will accompany those who believe: in my name they will cast out demons; they will speak with new languages; they will take up serpents; and if they drink any deadly thing, it will in no way hurt them; they will lay hands on the sick, and they will recover." (Mark 16:15–18)

In the commission that Christ gives in Mark 16, we are called to go into all the world and preach the good news. The word used for "world" is *cosmos*, which refers not merely to geography but also to peoples. My paraphrase of this verse is that God invites us to join him as he invades every sphere of our society and to preach the gospel in each of those spheres.

Then there is the Great Commission in Matthew:

> Jesus came to them and spoke to them, saying, "All authority has been given to me in heaven and on earth. Go, and

make disciples of all nations, baptizing them in the name of the Father and of the Son and of the Holy Spirit, teaching them to observe all things that I commanded you. Behold, I am with you always, even to the end of the age." Amen. (Matt. 28:18–20)

When the commission of Mark 16 is coupled with the commission of Matthew 28, we are called to disciple whole people groups, and by that I mean nations, language groups, cultural sub-groups, etc. To do that, we must enter into the worlds that they live in and not only preach the good news but also disciple entire communities until they become conformed to the image of Christ.

Compound Names of God

People sometimes think I am a bit extreme when I talk of discipling communities until they reflect Christ. I have often been accused of being an idealist. I now take that as a compliment.

All Christians would agree that man was originally created in the image and likeness of God and that even today we as individuals reflect something of the image of God, albeit somewhat distorted. What if this does not stop on an individual level? What if communities also reflect the image of the Godhead and each one of the spheres reveals something of the very nature and character of God?

Understanding the nature and character of God is only possible because God has chosen to reveal himself to us. Moses came across the burning bush, and God sent him on a mission. When Moses asked God his name, God revealed himself as "I AM."

Moses said to God, "Behold, when I come to the children of Israel, and tell them, 'The God of your fathers has sent me to you;' and they ask me, 'What is his name?' What should I tell them?" God said to Moses, "I AM WHO I AM," and he said, "You shall tell the children of Israel this: 'I AM has sent me to you.'" (Exod. 3:13–14)

It is from this name, translated as "I AM," that we get the name "Yahweh," which is an educated guess as to the pronunciation of YHWH, the Hebrew spelling of God's name. This name, known as the Tetragrammaton, is without vowels because Jews eventually considered the name of God to be too holy to utter. So instead of pronouncing the Tetragrammaton when they came across it in a text, they would say "Adonai," which means Lord.

This name Yahweh, as I will choose to write it, is not used just once in the Old Testament but is used many times. In many English translations, whenever you see LORD in capital letters, it indicates the use of that name.

God further reveals himself using that name in what are commonly called the compound names of God. Some of you may be familiar with the phrase "Jehovah (that is, Yahweh) Jireh," meaning "the Lord our provider" or "the Lord-seeing." When we take Yahweh to mean "I AM," we realize that God is revealing himself in a distinct way; he is saying, "I AM the one who sees." He sees our needs and he provides. This name for God gives us insight into the nature and character of God: he is someone who cares enough to see the needs of his children and provide for them.

I have found that it is possible to relate the different spheres of society to the compound names of God in the Old Testament. Why would I want to do this, you may ask? Well, simply because I have decided that what I believe and teach should be grounded in who God is. Once I realized that the spheres of society actually represent something of who God is, I came to believe that we have a responsibility to redeem societies and not just individuals.

So now I would like to take you on a rather abbreviated journey to show you the connection between the compound names of God and the spheres of our society and how I believe we can begin to reclaim lost ground. I will not be sticking strictly to the spheres mentioned above; I am adding military, law and government (in addition to government in general), rallying points, and wholeness.

Yahweh Elyon—government and politics

> Abram said to the king of Sodom, "I have lifted up my hand to Yahweh, God Most High, possessor of heaven and earth." (Gen. 14:22)

The first compound name of God that I would like to address is Yahweh Elyon, found in Genesis 14:22. This could be translated as "I AM the most high." In the Bible there is always hierarchy and authority when God is involved. The statement "I AM the most high" says two things to me: firstly, it speaks of the fact that there is an order of things; and secondly, it says that God is at the top of that order. Having governing authorities is not a man-made idea but a God-ordained concept.

Paul strongly supports the idea that governing authorities come from God:

> Let every soul be in subjection to the higher authorities, for there is no authority except from God, and those who exist

are ordained by God. Therefore he who resists the authority, withstands the ordinance of God; and those who withstand will receive to themselves judgment. For rulers are not a terror to the good work, but to the evil. Do you desire to have no fear of the authority? Do that which is good, and you will have praise from the same, for he is a servant of God to you for good. But if you do that which is evil, be afraid, for he doesn't bear the sword in vain; for he is a servant of God, an avenger for wrath to him who does evil. Therefore you need to be in subjection, not only because of the wrath, but also for conscience' sake. (Rom. 13:1–5)

Because God ordained government and this reflects something of who he is, I believe he is grieved when he sees the kinds of corrupt governments and politicians that exist today. In Sierra Leone the Anti-Corruption Commission uncovered that hundreds of millions of dollars were siphoned by politicians and ended up in their own personal accounts. This is money that should have gone toward basics like education, healthcare, and food. Would it then not make sense that the Great Commission is calling us to enter into the realm of government to preach the gospel and make disciples of individuals and help form a government that reflects God's purposes? A government reflecting God's purposes would affirm its people's human rights. It would care for the people instead of exploiting then. It would protect them instead of abusing them. It would not be stealing money for personal gain while the nation—to use Sierra Leone as an example—remains at the bottom of the 2007/2008 United Nations Human Development Index.

Yahweh Jireh—business and economics

> Abraham called the name of that place Yahweh Will Provide [Yahweh Jireh]. As it is said to this day, "On Yahweh's mountain, it will be provided." (Gen. 22:14)

Many Christians find the idea of God as our provider very comforting. God provides for us in many ways, and one of the ways is through businesses and the money they generate and the jobs they create. "But you shall remember Yahweh your God, for it is he who gives you power to get wealth; that he may establish his covenant which he swore to your fathers, as at this day" (Deut. 8:18). When I first read this passage, I was blown away. I had thought of business as such a worldly thing that it had never occurred to me that the ability to make money was a God-given gift. If we look around at our world, we will find that God has clearly gifted some people to run businesses. Sometimes these people are extraordinary entrepreneurs. Take Richard Branson of Virgin. He started his business from scratch and is now a major shareholder of a significant business empire.

The power to gain wealth is a gift from God that can be used for his glory or for selfish desires. All around us today we are surrounded by greed. Instead of people using businesses to provide income for many people, a few selfish people want it all to themselves. If businesses were being run as God intended, there would be no such thing as sweatshops in Malaysia where little kids manufacture products in terrible conditions for large multinationals. I am not against large companies, but I do believe greed has caused people to lose their way.

God desires a world where none go hungry because of other people's greed. Who will show the corporations of the world the plans and purposes of God? As Christians it is our responsibility to disciple the business world. It is part of the *cosmos* that God is sending us into.

Yahweh Rapha—health, science, and technology

And he said, "If you will diligently listen to the voice of Yahweh your God, and will do that which is right in his eyes, and will pay attention to his commandments, and keep all his statutes, I will put none of the diseases on you, which I have put on the Egyptians; for I am Yahweh who heals you." (Exod. 15:26)

We need to understand that God is our healer on two levels: the natural level and the supernatural level. When we look at the Old Testament, we see that God has made provision for our health and general welfare in practical ways. When these ways fail us, then we need supernatural intervention.

God taught the Israelites many things to increase their quality of life, and improving quality of life is meant to be the purpose of science and technology. For example, God gave the Israelites laws that improved the area of disease prevention. In the book of Leviticus, the people learn to separate people with communicable diseases from the rest of the population. They also learn how to deal with sewage by burying it as opposed to having it open in the middle of inhabited areas. It's shocking that some people today still do not know these simple truths, and the Bible could teach them all these things.

It is also fascinating how many medicines exist naturally in our world. We have all heard of the healing properties of garlic, for example. We also know that spicy foods are good for us because of the ability of capsaicin, found in hot peppers, to fight viruses. I am a big fan of echinacea to boost my immune

UP

DOWN

IN

OUT

system whenever I feel a cold coming on. Even the pharmaceutical industry creates many of its medicines from natural plants and herbs.

God has indeed made provisions for health in the very world in which we live. But it seems to me that people whom God has gifted with the ability to enhance health and quality of life have lost their way. The pharmaceutical industry is more concerned about making money than healing people. Doctors in some nations will not even touch a dying person until they see cash. The film *The Constant Gardener* depicts a pharmaceutical industry that is well and truly corrupt: instead of saving lives, the industry uses the less fortunate as guinea pigs for its next money-spinning drug.

Who will help God restore his purpose for health and healing and quality of life in our world? This task will have to be taken up by Christians. We must show the world God's heart for his people to be in health.

As Christians we also have the added advantage of the Holy Spirit's power to heal. Imagine if Christians around the world began to move in the kind of power that Jesus displayed on earth and promised that we would inherit (Eph. 1:19). Imagine seeing sickness and disease being pushed back. This can be a reality, and we can be a part of it.

Yahweh M'Kaddesh—religion and spirituality

> Speak also to the children of Israel, saying, "Most certainly you shall keep my Sabbaths: for it is a sign between me and you throughout your generations; that you may know that I am Yahweh who sanctifies you." (Exod. 31:13)

In this name, Yahweh M'Kaddesh, God declares himself to be our Sanctifier, the one who sets us apart from our sin and makes us clean—or to put it another way, the one who makes us holy. Part of how God chooses to sanctify Israel is by their observing of a Sabbath rest. Although I don't fully understand how this works, it definitely speaks to me about grace. By having to rest one day each week, we are reminded that it is not through our own work but the work of Christ that we experience sanctification. It is God himself who is our sanctifier.

Every society on earth tends toward some kind of religious activity or belief system. As Voltaire once said, "If God did not exist, it would be necessary to invent him." Voltaire recognized the innate tendency for human beings to worship or pay homage to something beyond them. Religion is a natural part of being human. At the heart of most religions are things like a desire to connect with God or gods, a desire to somehow make yourself right, or matters to do with the afterlife.

In my opinion, the primary drive behind religion for many people is to feel clean or acceptable, to feel that we make the grade. Whether this is accomplished by sacrificing animals or going on pilgrimage, religious people all tend toward being acceptable to their God or gods or perhaps in some cases themselves. This natural tendency is something that God has placed in us, and God is the only one who can truly fulfill that desire to be clean.

The process of sanctification, that is to say, of being made holy or clean, is one that only God, by his Spirit, can work in us. The vessel that God has chosen to use for this job is his body, the church. Thanks to what Christ has done and the discipline of the Father and the work of the Holy Spirit, we can share in God's holiness (Heb. 12:10).

I also believe that God has designed his children to help one another grow into Christlikeness. Becoming Christlike would be my very simple way of describing the process of sanctification.

God has called some people to focus on this job of sanctification. These people are involved in leading, teaching, and all kinds of ministries that facilitate the process of sanctification. For example, a teacher will help us see how to live the Christian life or a prophet might bring a word of correction about sin in our lives. Looking at the Old Testament, we see that God separated, or sanctified, the Levites to minister sanctification to the rest of the nation of Israel; it was the Levites who made the offerings and ran the temple. Today the Lord has done away with burnt offerings and the like because of the finished work of the Cross. God's chosen method of sanctification has changed, but that does not mean he no longer desires certain people to help others find holiness. The church flows from the very heart of God; it flows from who he is, and he is the Sanctifier.

Yahweh Rohi—education and media

Yahweh is my shepherd: I shall lack nothing. (Ps. 23:1)

In this name, Yahweh Rohi, God declares himself to be the one who shepherds us. In the New Testament Christ is called the shepherd of our souls: "For you were going astray like sheep; but now have returned to the Shepherd and Overseer of your souls" (1 Pet. 2:25).

In the twenty-third Psalm, the shepherd has many roles. These range from protecting the sheep to guiding them. Within the Christian context, we often see leaders, especially pastors and teachers, as shepherds too. Christ is the chief shepherd, and they are under him (1 Pet. 5:2–4) They are the ones who guide us and help shape us and disciple us into our true identity in Christ. The twofold question we have to ask ourselves today is, who is shepherding us? and more important, who is shepherding our children?

The role of shepherding children has presently been given over to our schools. Many children spend more time at school and other educational institutions than they spend with their parents. Another shepherd out there, which some of us are less aware of, is the media. If you look around today, it is not hard to see that the media plays a major role in shaping how young people dress and think and what they value. This occurs not only through well-thought-through marketing campaigns but even through less obvious means such as news items and movies. Values are communicated through media that young people end up adopting.

God, our ultimate Shepherd, wants to shape us according to his values. It is therefore important that as Christians we do not have a laissez-faire approach to the educational system and media but instead make sure that what is shaping our children and our world is in accordance with the desires and purposes of God. I do not for one moment think of our media or educational systems as evil. Like many things in our world, they can be used to further God's purposes *or* the devil's purposes, and we can make a difference as to how these tools are used to shape our world. I believe that our schools and our media can become powerful tools in the hands of God.

Yahweh Hosenu—arts, entertainment, and sports

Oh come, let's worship and bow down. Let's kneel before Yahweh, our Maker. (Ps. 95:6)

With this name, Yahweh Hosenu, God declares himself to be our Creator. If you are like me, then you normally think about God's creating from a scientific point of view, in that God is the one who brought us into being. Reconsidering the word *maker* or the word *creator*, however, I recognize that creating this planet and all that is on it was not merely an engineering exercise for God but was an artistic process as well.

Have you ever paused to enjoy all the vibrant colors around you? The flowers, the sky, a green field, the forests. This world was created not simply by an inventor but by an artist. The appreciation of beauty is something that we have inherited from God. Think of how much time humans spend enjoying, doing, or creating things that achieve nothing functional but stimulate their senses and give them pleasure. Think of the latest Hollywood film, an opera, a game of basketball, or a visit to an art gallery. These things have one thing in common: intrinsic pleasure and enjoyment. The point is to enjoy beauty for beauty's sake. Although I believe that there is a danger of becoming worshipers of entertainment, I also believe that the whole sphere of arts and entertainment is born out of the very heart of God. He is a creator and an enjoyer of things that he created. It comes as no surprise, then, that we are the same.

As with many of the other spheres of our society, human depravity has taken its toll. I don't need to go into much detail, but if you think about the filth that comes out of the film industry or the ridiculous specimens people try to pass off as art today, you will know what I mean.

God wants our creativity to reflect his nature. By this I am not implying that every song has to be about Jesus or every painting has to depict Christ or some other biblical scene. On the contrary, I am saying let's paint and sing and make movies about whatever we want. Let's just make sure that the values of whatever we create reflect those of our God. Instead of promoting promiscuity as a virtue as many TV programs do, for example, we ought to promote sexual purity as a virtue. This does not mean that we avoid reality and pretend that issues of sin and depravity don't exist in our world. We must face the reality of our world and present God's values as the ultimate reality and the ultimate form of creativity and beauty.

Yahweh Shammah—family and community

> It shall be eighteen thousand reeds around: and the name of the city from that day shall be, Yahweh is there. (Ezek. 48:35)

This compound name of God sums up much of what is being said in this chapter. Yahweh Shammah is God's declaration that "I AM there." In the midst of suffering and joy, through love and pain, God is present. This is the voice not merely of a Supreme Being but of a Father.

Our Father in heaven says to us that he is present in our midst. In a world where many children grow up without fathers, this is a powerful statement showing that God is a relational God who promotes family and community. The verse in Ezekiel comes after a wonderful description of the city of God that awaits us. It shows us that God is building a community of people that he will not only be present in but be the very center of.

Families and communities today are but a shadow of God's purposes for family and community. Because the Trinity is a family and community of love, we can learn from the Trinity about how families and communities are meant to be. Our world is full of broken families ravaged by abuse and divorce and other such invaders that have no place in family life. God has called us as Christians to model family and community life. Families and communities can be strong only through love, and we know that God is love. Let us soak ourselves in the love of God so much that the world cannot help but learn from us about how

God desires and intends family and community to be. Let all of us seek to model the very nature of God—the ever present and ever loving One—in our homes and our communities.

Yahweh Nissi—rallying points

Moses built an altar, and called its name Yahweh our Banner. (Exod. 17:15)

The Lord declares himself to be the banner of Israel. The banner was the rallying point of the nation at the start of war; it is where they gathered together to find strength. The name Yahweh Nissi is not an easy name to fit neatly into the framework of the spheres, so I won't try to make it fit neatly. But I will share a few ideas of how this name relates to our world. See what you think.

Humans love to gather together in one place or for one purpose. The desire to gather is natural. We like to discover our commonalities and allow them to unite us. That is why we have so many social clubs, pubs, and parties. I believe it is God's heart that we gather together and bless and encourage one another.

In his book *The Great Good Place,* sociologist Ray Oldenburg presented the concept of the "third place." The subtitle of the book hints at his argument: *Cafes, Coffee Shops, Community Centers, Beauty Parlors, General Stores, Bars, Hangouts and How They Get You Through the Day.* Oldenburg observes three places where people find themselves: their homes, their workplace, and the "third place." The third place is where people choose to go to relax and be with friends and other people who have shared life and experiences with them. Remember the old sitcom *Cheers?* The bar was a place for people to go "where everybody knows your name." It was a third place.

Many people are in the business of providing the third place. Cafes, nightclubs, and pubs are all third places—places where people can find security, safety, and a sense of belonging. Not all third places today are wholesome and healthy, promoting a real sense of security and safety. Many nightclubs, for example, have become meat markets where people pick up one-night stands. It is easy for someone to think they can find love and acceptance in such a place, but in many cases this thin veneer gives way to a more painful reality that we still do not belong, or worse still, that we have been used.

God, I believe, is our ultimate third place. Psalm 16:11 states, "You will show me the path of life. In your presence is fullness of joy. In your right hand there are pleasures forevermore." Because God is the source of life, joy, and pleasure, Christians have an opportunity to provide third places that are centered on God and his values. In many places where I have lived, I have heard constant complaints about there being nowhere for youth to hang out. I know of a handful of ministries in the UK that are impacting their communities by providing a third place for people to come to and have many of their social needs met. Would it not be wonderful if more Christians facilitated the development of safe third places with wholesome atmospheres?

Yahweh Sabbaoth—military and warfare

In the year that king Uzziah died, I saw the Lord sitting on a throne, high and lifted up; and his train filled the temple. Above him stood the seraphim. Each one had six wings. With two he covered his face. With two he covered his feet. With two he flew. One called to another, and said, "Holy, holy, holy, is Yahweh of Armies! The whole earth is full of his glory!" (Isa. 6:1–3)

UP

DOWN

IN

OUT

The name Yahweh Sabbaoth is one of the most commonly used names of God in the Bible (it is found over 250 times in the Old Testament) and can be translated as "Lord of Hosts," as in the angelic hosts of heaven. To be honest, this scares me. Why? Because "hosts" is primarily a military term. Basically God calls himself the Lord of heaven's armies over 250 times. Although this will make the pacifists uncomfortable, I have to say that we cannot escape the fact that our God is a warrior God. Of course, God's *whole* identity is not tied up in this name, but the name is still very much a *part* of his identity. He is a God who shamelessly declares that he leads an army. And if God leads an army, is it any surprise that humans have armies too?

Is it possible, then, that the fact that most nations have an army is a reflection of the Lord of Hosts? This is a difficult question. Personally, I have to consider that there is a place for the military in our society even though I am mostly pacifist in my thinking. If its purpose is not to create war, then at least the military can act as a deterrent to those who would seek to oppress the weak. When we consider the Second World War, for example, most of us are grateful that many men and women gave their lives for the defense of the defenseless.

I concede that many armies have been used to fight unjust wars or to prey on the weak. This does not deter me from recognizing the legitimacy of the military but confirms for me the idea that the armies of our world desperately need to reflect the heart of God. They need to make defending the defenseless their primary objective. The purpose of an army might not be to attack but to defend a nation against unscrupulous villains.

We live in a world with armies. It could be that armies are born out of the heart of God. We know that armies have been responsible for many atrocities in our world, but on many occasions they have also protected the vulnerable. While we need to pray for the ideal scenario where armies don't need to exist, we are faced with a present reality that we cannot ignore. With this in mind, I pray that God raises more and more God-fearing leaders in our military so that we can one day boast of having an army whose role is to serve God's purposes.

Yahweh Tsidkenu—law and government

In his days Judah shall be saved, and Israel shall dwell safely; and this is his name by which he shall be called: Yahweh our righteousness. (Jer. 23:6)

With this name, Yahweh Tsidkenu, God declares himself to be our righteousness. I learned from a mentor that this word we translate as "righteousness" can also be translated as "justice." God is not only our righteousness in the sense of salvation, but he is also our justice. We know from the Scriptures that through Christ we have died to sin and live to righteousness (1 Pet. 2:24); however, many of us are not yet familiar with the idea of our God being our justice.

God's justice often comes under question as people struggle to make sense of injustices in our world, especially when some of our theologies ascribe the cause of these injustices to God. Has it ever occurred to you that the strong sense of anger we feel against injustice is something that is born of God? The fact that we have courts and police to uphold justice is not by mere chance but is another example of God's nature and character being reflected in our world.

It breaks my heart to see corrupt justice systems in the world. Money seems to determine who will win a court case these days. In my birth nation of Sierra Leone the corruption in the justice system is so bad that you can bribe your way out of many crimes. I myself have been guilty in the past of using money to get away with a driving offense.

Many of us have friends who are lawyers or policemen. Would we not desire that these friends be able to shine the light of Christ in their workplace? Do we not dream that they would join the battle against injustice, that they would stand up for truth and not simply go with the flow? God's heart for justice must shine through our judicial system. It must be restored to the purpose that God intended.

Yahweh Shalom—wholeness

> Then Gideon built an altar there to Yahweh, and called it "Yahweh is Peace." To this day it is yet in Ophrah of the Abiezrites. (Judg. 6:24)

Yahweh Shalom, "I AM your peace," is what the Lord declares here. Often when we hear the word *peace,* we associate it with the absence of war. The Jewish idea of peace, however, entails a lot more than that. *Shalom* is more like the kind of peace of mind that comes with prosperity and wholeness and being at peace with your neighbors. God calls us to this kind of peace. He himself is our peace and our wholeness, and our desire for peace and wholeness comes from him.

Many people today have lost their peace of mind. More and more social workers, psychologists, and community workers are trying to help people find shalom. I believe God is at work in this world through the lives of such workers. He wants not just individuals but whole communities to find shalom. He calls us to minister to the broken hearted, the mentally ill, the deprived, the orphaned, and the less fortunate in our world. He desires that we would join him in his quest to restore wholeness in the world.

Christians have encountered the peace of God that can be fully experienced through the cross of Christ. Who better to show the world that it is possible to find shalom even when conflict surrounds us?

Making Disciples

At the end of this chapter some of you may be thinking, *He doesn't really believe that the spheres of our fallen world come out of the heart of God, does he?* I most certainly do. I see humanity as an imperfect reflection of a perfect God who desires to restore us to the perfection that is available to us in Christ.

Some of you may also want to dismiss my thoughts in this chapter as rather tenuous links between God's names and the spheres of society to make points that could be made in a much easier way. That has not been my aim. My aim has been to show you a different way of looking at the world around us by focusing on the positive and redeemable aspects of our society and on how we can take responsibility for shaping it. I want to help people find meaning in their life and work and realize that they are ministers of God regardless of their job. Whether they are at home ministering God's heart for family or in an office ministering God's heart for good business or government, it doesn't matter.

As we grasp this, the idea of making disciples throughout the entire world becomes bigger and more intimidating but also more accessible to each of us. We will no longer see disciple making as the sole work of pastors and missionaries but as a task that the whole church is involved in. Instead of seeing discipleship as a task that occurs at church meetings, house groups, or baptismal classes, it becomes a process that takes place all day every day, everywhere we go. We can join hands with God in discipling the world and transforming it into the image of Christ.

Without a doubt, one of the greatest challenges the average Christian faces is reaching out to others. If you are like me, the word *evangelism* can sometimes strike fear into the very center of your being. We often think of stereotypical evangelism scenarios such as knocking on doors or standing on the street shouting at people. I have engaged in both of these activities and seen them bear fruit, but I would not call them evangelism. I would call door knocking and street preaching tools or methods of evangelism.

Evangelism itself has a much simpler definition. It is the proclamation of the good news of the kingdom of God. If evangelism is this simple (note that I did not say *easy*), then surely we can all engage in some form of evangelism. How? Well, that's the million dollar question that I would like to give my perspective on in a rather roundabout way.

Christ As a Model

As I have grown in my faith, I have looked to others as role models but have sometimes ignored the most obvious role model: Jesus. Jesus has much to teach us about evangelism. The Gospels state that one of Jesus' main tasks was to preach the good news. In Luke 4, Jesus starts his ministry with a declaration from Isaiah 61 that leaves us with no doubt about his intentions: he was anointed to preach good news to the poor (Luke 4:18).

The next question that comes to mind is, what is this good news that Jesus came to preach? In the Gospels this good news takes many forms. John talks about eternal life, Matthew talks mainly about the kingdom of heaven but also the kingdom of God, and Mark and Luke talk about the kingdom of God. All these are pointing to a new era with new possibilities for how man can relate to God and his kingdom. Whatever way we look at it, the kingdom is very much related to God. John defines eternal life as knowing God, and the Synoptic Gospel references to the kingdom of God inescapably link the kingdom to God. Taking John's definition of eternal life (John 17:3), we realize that relationship with God is at the heart of evangelism.

It is for this reason that I believe the central purpose of evangelism is reconciliation with God. Through reconciliation with God, we can experience some of the other results that Jesus mentions in Luke 4. It is through a restored relationship that blind eyes will be opened, captives will be set free, and broken hearts will be bound up (Luke 4:18–19). Sometimes people focus solely on the saving of souls, but in my opinion a saved soul is a natural by-product of a restored relationship with God.

> But all things are of God, who reconciled us to himself through Jesus Christ, and gave to us the ministry of reconciliation; namely, that God was in Christ reconciling the world to himself, not reckoning to them their trespasses,

and having committed to us the word of reconciliation. (2 Cor. 5:18–19)

This scripture shows us that the ministry of reconciliation started not with us but with God. What we do is join God in a task that has been going on for a long time. Jesus' incarnational life began a new covenant and a new ministry of reconciliation, his death made true reconciliation possible, and his resurrection enforced its reality.

We should always be asking ourselves the question, what can I learn from Jesus? Since Christ played a major role in this ministry of reconciliation, we can learn much from him and follow his example. Three key words to describe the ministry of Jesus are *incarnation, crucifixion,* and *resurrection.* I believe these three words can be used as structure for thinking about evangelism.

Motivation

But before I delve into these three areas, I want to highlight the starting point for any kind of kingdom ministry: our motivations.

God in his grace has convicted me on many occasions of wrong motivations for reaching out to others. In evangelism there is a danger of falling into the traps of legalism, selfish ambition, and our own guilt, to name a few. Any time we fall into one of these traps, we have lost sight of the true motive for evangelism.

When we look at Jesus, we find that the main driving force behind his ministry was love and compassion. John 3:16 is very clear: it is because God loved the world that he sent his only

Son. Therefore it is love that compels us to reach out. "For the love of Christ constrains us; because we judge thus, that one died for all, therefore all died" (2 Cor. 5:14).

It is my sincere belief that the primary motivation for kingdom ministry should always be love—love for God that leads to obedience, and love for one another that births compassion. In both ways the root is love. Let's look at these two motivations, compassion and obedience, to be in the ministry of reconciliation.

As I look back on my life, I can see many times when I reached out to others for the wrong reasons. Sometimes I reached out to placate the sense of guilt that I felt. This kind of guilt-born evangelism is one that many of us experience, especially if we work for churches or ministries. If nothing else, we feel like we have to evangelize because it's our job. This is a selfish approach to evangelism, because it's not really about loving our neighbor; it's more about fulfilling our duty and feeling better about ourselves. We need to ask God to pour his compassion into us to move and motivate us to Christlikeness, which involves meeting needs, not just challenging people to repent of their sins.

When Jesus ministered on the earth, often the thing that triggered his action was his compassion and love for people. Jesus healed the sick out of compassion (Matt. 14:14). He opened blind eyes out of compassion (Matt. 20:34). He had compassion on the multitude because they had nothing to eat (Matt. 15:32). Even his teaching was born out of compassion (Mark 6:34).

Jesus also ministered out of obedience. He did only what he saw his Father doing, and we are called to join the Father in reaching out into a broken and disobedient world. Doing this is not optional but is actually at the heart of what we are called to be as Christians. It would violate the purpose and heart of God for us to become dead ends for grace. God in his wisdom has embedded a command right from the start to reach out to others within the good news. Like Abraham we have been blessed to be a blessing. God's wonderful promise to Abraham in Genesis 12 is focused not so much on Abraham's needs but on the needs of the whole world.

When Jesus sent out his disciples, he gave them a similar command to the one given to Abraham: "Heal the sick, cleanse the lepers, and cast out demons. Freely you received, so freely give" (Matt. 10:8). Jesus also said to his disciples, in Matthew 28:20, that they were to teach the nations—that includes us—to obey all that he commanded them. Therefore the command to freely give as we have received is one that applies to anyone who calls himself or herself a follower of Christ. And commands are there to be obeyed; they are not mere suggestions.

Our ministries need to be birthed out of compassion for others and obedience to God. These two foundations will not easily be shaken. Any ministry with the right motivation will go the distance and can truly call itself a kingdom ministry.

Now that the issue of motivation has been addressed, I would like to pursue my threefold model of evangelism, namely, incarnation, crucifixion, and resurrection.

Incarnation

The first stage of Jesus' ministry of reconciliation was the Incarnation. The coming of God in fleshly form is one of the most remarkable moments of history. I still cannot fully get my head around the idea that God himself came to us. He did not send his angels or other help; he did the job personally. This incredible Being willingly limited himself by taking on human flesh, with all its vulnerabilities, to reach us. It was a step down to become human, and that was his plan and desire. Philippians 2:6–7 speaks of Christ, "who, existing in the form of God, didn't consider equality with God a thing to be grasped, but emptied himself, taking the form of a servant, being made in the likeness of men."

A significance of the Incarnation is this: Jesus knows how people feel and what they have experienced, because he has lived among us. We sometimes attempt to do evangelism from a distance, as if by remote control. People won't respond to our bombarding them with messages. They want to see the good news at work in our lives. The Word needs to be fleshed out.

The Bible calls us not simply to evangelize (spread the good news) but also to make disciples. Real evangelism, which includes the ministry of reconciliation, is about restoration of relationship, and the ultimate fulfillment of that comes when someone becomes a disciple of Jesus. A disciple does not merely subscribe to a set of theological beliefs but genuinely follows Jesus Christ in obedience. Learning obedience will take time and is something people will have to see fleshed out in our lives before they can really grasp it.

Jesus spent so much time with the "wrong" sorts of people that religious people made accusations about his morality. They said he was a friend of tax collectors and "sinners" (Matt. 11:19). He apparently spent so much time hanging out with such people that he was called a winebibber and a glutton. I bet Jesus was proud to be called a friend of sinners. He himself did not sin, but he was only too happy to be in the company of those who did. The physician is needed by those who are ill (Matt. 9:12).

Christians are called to imitate Christ and be present among those who need the Great Physician. Light is needed where there is darkness, and a society that is flavorless and rotting needs to be salted.

During my university days, there was a group of students who were unwilling to reach out to people in the pubs. This didn't make much sense to me. If God was willing to get his hands dirty by coming to this planet and facing temptation and being surrounded by the filth and muck of human sin and degradation, then we too should be willing to get our hands dirty by visiting some places we might perceive as unsavory for the sake of Jesus.

The challenge to be like Jesus has brought me to live in one of the toughest areas of Dundee called Hilltown. I used to live in the nice suburb areas with a house that had a lovely drive to park the car (which makes car insurance cheaper) and a view of the Tay River. But God started speaking to me. It was well and good that I lived a nice, comfortable life and worked in the ministry, but was I willing to go and live among the people that I claimed God loved and cared for? Hilltown has a high rate of teenage pregnancies, a major drug and alcohol problem, a high crime rate, and such violence that two people were stabbed two weeks before my family moved to the area.

Christians are called to be an embodiment of Christ's light and to display Christlikeness in the midst of darkness. How far are you willing to go? The idea of bringing people to meetings is different from Jesus' going to where the people were. Although it is uncomfortable, we must go and seek people where they are.

Jesus' incarnation is a challenge to me. He came to our world and hung out with prostitutes. I don't pretend that hanging out with prostitutes is easy, because it's not. But that's what "crucifixion," the next topic, is all about. It is being willing to do the things that are difficult and to make sacrifices.

Crucifixion

Martyrdom is a subject that has always fascinated and scared me at the same time. Some Christian traditions describe three types of martyrdom: red, white, and green. Red martyrdom is when a believer loses his or her life for the sake of Christ. White martyrdom is when a believer abandons all that he or she loves for the sake of Christ, often leaving behind homeland, friends, and family. And green martyrdom entails moving into the countryside or another remote place to live the life of a hermit with plenty of prayer and fasting.

Whichever way we look at martyrdom, one common thread between them is sacrifice. I believe that all Christians are called to some form of martyrdom. We can choose whatever color we want and even add our own tint. The main thing is the call to sacrifice. Since I have already discussed sacrifice in an earlier chapter, I won't labor the point here. I simply want to apply it to the context of evangelism.

As I mentioned before, God revealed to me in a 24/7 prayer room that many of us are not willing to suffer or choose sacrifice to see his kingdom come. Jesus was willing to die for his ministry of reconciliation. Being called to faith as a Christian is an invitation to sacrifice. We have to sacrifice our energy, our money, and sometimes, even harder, our comforts. In our Western culture we are so obsessed with comfort that when Christians face difficulty, they say it's an attack of the enemy. But Christ said, "If they persecuted me, they will also persecute you" (John 15:20).

We cannot make a difference in this world without it costing us something. Jesus was willing to die for his cause. In this day and age, there are many who seem willing to kill for their faith but few who will die for their faith. Those who kill for their faith will be remembered as cowards, but those who die for their faith in Christ will reign with him.

Sacrifice can be expressed in less drastic ways than martyrdom. There was a time when Jesus was trying to get some rest with his disciples, but the people around him had needs and he willingly gave up his time of rest to minister to them. This will happen to us, too. There will be times when we have plans for our days or evenings, but our neighbor or flatmate will have needs, and we will have to make sacrifices to meet those needs.

When I compare my life to Christ's, I realize that I have much work to do to reach the goal of becoming like Christ in every area, including reaching out to others. For example, I am not very extroverted, and I get intimidated by talking to strangers. But sometimes I have to put my shyness aside and go and talk to someone on the street or in a cafe. A couple of years ago I was on the streets asking people to help with a survey I was doing. As usual, I was incredibly nervous, but I felt like I had to be a good role model to the YWAM student who was with me. I eventually plucked up the courage and approached a young man. I had to lay aside my inhibitions and resist every instinct to run away. In the end it was not so hard, especially since the young guy was open to hearing what I had to say. We should not allow ourselves to become imprisoned by our personalities.

The good news for us is that no sacrifice made for Christ will go unrewarded. Christ himself received a reward for his sacrifice on the cross. He was resurrected to sit at the right hand of the Father and has received dominion over all things. This leads me to the subject of resurrection.

UP

DOWN

IN

OUT

Resurrection

There are many possible interpretations of the significance of Jesus' resurrection. Here is one: the Resurrection was a demonstration of the Holy Spirit's power. Just as Christ, who *is* God, was dependent on the Holy Spirit's power during his ministry on earth, we must depend on the Holy Spirit's power during our ministry. We need God's power to reach out. For us to try to reach out to others without the Spirit's power is folly. It will not bear fruit.

I would like to look at a passage from Romans to support my point.

> For I will not dare to speak of any things except those which Christ worked through me, for the obedience of the Gentiles, by word and deed, in the power of signs and wonders, in the power of God's Spirit; so that from Jerusalem, and around as far as to Illyricum, I have fully preached the Good News of Christ; yes, making it my aim to preach the Good News, not where Christ was already named, that I might not build on another's foundation. (Rom. 15:18–20)

Firstly, Paul states his goal in evangelism. Then he describes how he achieves this goal: by word and deed and in signs and wonders. Lastly, he points out that all of his actions operate through the Spirit's power. I would like to examine these key points from the passage.

The goal

Paul states that his goal in evangelism is to bring Gentiles into obedience to Christ. The point of evangelism and discipleship is not to get someone to say the sinner's prayer or make a commitment some other way so that we can tick a box; it is to lead a person to obedience. Obedience is what making disciples is about. It is sad that some people think evangelism is like the job of a salesperson: if we can only get people to sign on the dotted line, then we have them. The goal of the salesperson is to get commitments to buy, and the rest of the job—everything from accepting the payment for the product to teaching the buyer how to use it and maintain it—is left to the after-sales team. For Paul, however, the goal of preaching is to bring people into obedience. That is the true meaning of a disciple: someone who loves Jesus enough to obey him and strenuously attempts to do so.

Word and deed

Paul then describes *how* he preaches the gospel. He first mentions that he uses words. Without a doubt, an essential component of evangelism is actually talking to people about Christ. The Bible calls us to proclaim the good news of Christ, and there is no escaping the simple reality that we must make proclamations. As Romans 10:14 asks, "How will they hear without a preacher?"

But *our* words alone are not enough. While we must open our mouths and proclaim to others the good news of the kingdom so that they can hear and believe, we must bear in mind that different people respond in different ways to our words. We cannot succumb to the temptation of using formulas. We must ask God to give us the right words to use in each unique situation. It is amazing how Jesus never seems to repeat himself in the encounters he has with people.

Paul goes on to mention another component of the ministry of evangelism, namely, deeds. I believe that there are two

UP

DOWN

IN

OUT

kinds of deeds that affect the preaching of the gospel. The first is living out what we believe about righteousness so that we can be an example to people. The second is the opportunity to serve people's needs through mercy ministry and social action.

In the stories about Jesus, one thing that always stands out to me is how his life was such a perfect example to everyone around. The Pharisees struggled to find moral failings on Jesus' part to attack him, so in the end they attacked him primarily on a theological basis, for claiming to be the Son of God. One of the major complaints we hear from unbelievers is that Christians are hypocrites. In their opinion we claim to have a higher moral standard, but in reality they do not see much difference between us and the rest of society. Although I do not believe this is entirely true, I think it is important to take notice of what is being said. Something about how we live our lives leaves unbelievers thoroughly unimpressed.

I also observe that Jesus was in the business of meeting people's needs. He had what we might call today a "holistic ministry," in which he met people's physical, spiritual, and emotional needs. When there was a group of hungry people, he fed them. When there were people with physical illnesses, he healed them. When there were hypocritical Pharisees, he rebuked them and showed them the truth about their spiritual condition. He was always identifying people's needs and meeting them as the Spirit led him.

I have been inspired by the diversity of ministries all over the world meeting the needs of the homeless, orphans, youth, the sick, and prisoners. This has been a long part of Christian history, and long may it continue. I once heard someone say, "People don't care what you know until they know that you care." I believe mercy ministry is one of the ways in which we can show our care for the world today, especially to the postmodern generation.

Signs and wonders

In the Romans passage, Paul adds that the ministry of evangelism is expressed through signs and wonders. Signs and wonders are an important part of the New Testament ministry of reaching the lost. Many times when Jesus was meeting the needs of people he actually used supernatural means. In one case people came to faith in Jesus because they concluded that the Messiah was not going to do more signs than Jesus had already done: "But of the multitude, many believed in him. They said, 'When the Christ comes, he won't do more signs than those which this man has done, will he?'" (John 7:31).

Even Jesus' disciples were influenced by his miracles when they chose to follow him. John says that it was after the miracle at the wedding that his glory was revealed and his disciples believed in him. "This beginning of his signs Jesus did in Cana of Galilee, and revealed his glory; and his disciples believed in him" (John 2:11).

Although signs alone will not bring people to faith in Christ, they certainly help. I have observed that in places like China and some parts of Africa where Christianity is growing at a fast rate, there are also reports of miracles. For example, Iris Ministries of Mozambique has planted thousands of churches, and they regularly report healings. I pray that all Christians, wherever they are, would see an increase in the release of signs and wonders so that we may more effectively bring people into obedience to Jesus.

Whether or not you believe that miracles happen today, you should agree that the process of someone being transformed into a new creation, being taken from darkness into light, is miraculous. This transformation is not something that can be accomplished by human effort. It is accomplished only by the power of God, and it's an incredible miracle.

The Spirit's power

Paul says that all of his ministry is done in the Spirit's power. We cannot overstate our dependence on the Holy Spirit in evangelism. The same Spirit who raised Christ from the dead is available to us today to make our evangelism effective (Rom. 8:11). One of the ways our dependence on the Spirit's power can be manifested is in our prayer life.

Several years ago I learned firsthand the value of prayer in reaching the lost. I had been reading a book called *Intercessory Prayer* by Dutch Sheets, and in one chapter he talked about how we can pray for those who don't yet know Jesus. He pointed out that since becoming born-again is a creative work of the Holy Spirit, we can use the creation story in Genesis to inspire our prayers. The bottom line was that we can ask the Holy Spirit to hover over people's lives and bring new life out of the chaos of an unregenerate life.

Being the skeptic that I sometimes am, I wanted to put this idea to the test. I had a friend who was keen to have her flatmate find faith in Jesus but had been met with resistance on many occasions. The flatmate refused to visit church gatherings or anything like that with my friend. I decided that this girl, call her Jane, would be my candidate for the experiment. I cheekily (and rather arrogantly) told my friend that I intended to have more success in sharing Christ with Jane than she had experienced so far. So I started praying for Jane like Dutch Sheets had suggested, and after a few days I invited her to a Christian meeting. She came. Next she agreed to do an Alpha course. The long and short of the story is that within a few months Jane had completed an Alpha course, given her life to the Lord, and received the baptism of the Holy Spirit. To be honest, we were all a bit taken aback, but we knew that all that had happened could be put down to the power of prayer. I must admit that I don't know how Jane is doing in her faith today, because she graduated from university and went her separate way. I knew that at some point before she graduated, she was struggling, but I continue to pray that things are going well for her. The point of this story is to illustrate how powerful prayer can be in the journey from unbeliever to believer.

Recently God has challenged me about losing my belief in the effectiveness of prayer, because if I did believe in it, I would spend more time praying than I presently do. Our behavior never lies. Our values are displayed outwardly by our behavior regardless of what we claim to believe. If I really believe that prayer is necessary for reaching out, then I will pray more.

The Harvest Is Plentiful

I am aware that many people get discouraged by evangelism because they believe it yields limited fruit and therefore see no point to it. I would like to encourage you not to give up by sharing a little story.

Several years ago I was doing a summer program in London that involved lectures in the morning and outreach in the afternoon. One lecture expounded on Matthew 9:37–38: "Then he said to his disciples, 'The harvest indeed is plentiful, but the laborers are few. Pray therefore that the Lord of the harvest will send out laborers into his harvest.'" As I came away from the lecture, I asked the Lord why so few people were following Christ if the harvest was really out there. It was one of those times when I challenged God to prove his word to me. (This might not be the recommended approach, but it has worked for me on a few occasions.) To my surprise, God was to prove himself to me that very afternoon.

On our training schedule, all the students were supposed to go door knocking. At one point during the door knocking, I again challenged the Lord to prove his word. At the next door that my friend and I knocked on, there was a young man who listened attentively to what we had to say, and he told us that his grandma was a Christian and had been sharing her faith with him. This young man was so receptive I was blown away; it seemed too good to be true. So I kept making my message more and more challenging to test him. I even tried to freak him out by telling him about baptism in the Holy Spirit. Still he was unmoved, and he wanted to make a commitment to Christ. I was still so shocked and suspicious that I told him that we would go away for twenty minutes or so to give him time to think about what he was about to do, because it was very serious business. Off we went, and when we came back half an hour later, he was still determined to make a commitment. In the end we led him in a prayer of faith and commitment to Christ and asked the Lord to fill him with his Spirit. This, I believe, marked the start of a discipleship journey for him.

God used this situation to show me that the fields are truly white unto harvest. We just need to find the people out there who are ready to take the next step on their spiritual journey.

This leaves me with little excuse for not somehow reaching out to the world around me. The same is true for you. Are you willing to play your part in God's master plan for reconciliation, or will you sit on the bench watching to see what happens? The choice is yours.

UP

DOWN

IN

OUT

11. The Spheres of Society
12. Evangelism Jesus-Style
13. Reaching Postmoderns

There is talk about postmodernity almost everywhere we look today. In the previous chapter I gave some general principles that I believe are useful in reaching out to the world around us; and because they are general, I believe those principles can be applied to people of any place, language, and culture. In this chapter I would like to highlight some points for people like myself who are living specifically in a postmodern context and want to reach out.

Earlier I pointed out that a major shift is happening in the West from a modern worldview to a postmodern worldview. If we take this shift into consideration, it would make sense that the eternal gospel which we proclaim must now be presented in a way that this postmodern generation can understand. Although the core content of the message has not and will not change, how the message is presented will vary.

In my opinion, trying to speak to postmoderns using modernist methods is like preaching the gospel to a Korean using Swahili. No matter how passionate you are about your message or how powerful and true it is, that doesn't change the fact that the recipient of the message can do little with it if he or she can't understand it.

We might assume that because someone speaks the same language as us, we will be able to understand what they are saying. But even if someone is speaking our language, we still might not understand what they are saying. If, for example, a geophysicist tried to explain something to me using highly technical language, I would understand very little. Similarly, a lot of the words that Christians use are not used all that much outside of a Christian context. So, when speaking to postmoderns who are unfamiliar with Christianity, we will achieve little in the way of genuine communication by sharing the good news of Christ using modern language and unfamiliar Christian terms.

Therefore it is my belief that we need to understand some of the basic differences between modern and postmodern ways of thinking so that we can communicate effectively. Defining modernity and postmodernity is not an easy thing to do. However, I will try to give some general ideas about each so that a reasonable comparison can be made to help identify ways in which we can customize our preaching of the gospel.

Truth and Assumptions

In many ways the origin of modernity is tied up with the exploration of truth. Some people suggest that the birth of modernism came through Rene Descartes, who attempted to evangelize people without using God as his staring point but instead using shared assumptions about truth and methods that philosophers in his day were familiar with.

A modernist way of looking at truth is that it is knowable by humans and that it is objective. Truth must be rationalized and

UP

reasoned out until we find absolute truth, which is applicable to every person everywhere because truth is a description of objective reality. A good example of an objective truth is gravity. Whether we like it or not, modernist or postmodernist, we are all subject to gravity, regardless of our background or culture.

DOWN

In modernity, the assumption is made that we can get better and better at working out truth, and as we do this, we can improve ourselves as a race. There is an emphasis on the experimental process, where truth is acquired by collecting data that is available to us through our senses. This way of thinking makes it difficult to entertain any thoughts of a supernatural world because it cannot easily be perceived by the senses or measured. Some of the key words that come to mind to sum up modernity are *rationalism, absolute truth, mechanical,* and *systematic.*

Postmodernity challenges many of modernity's assumptions. I would first like to highlight that postmodernity challenges the reliability of human perception and does not trust that as humans we are able to perceive truth in its entirety.

IN

This leads postmoderns to question whether there *is* objective truth that we have inerrant access to. A postmodern might say that even if there were absolute truth, we would not be able to be objective enough or have perceptions reliable enough to uncover it. For example, if we take what some might call an absolute measurement such as temperature, a postmodern might argue that a human still has to read the thermometer and the person might have an eyesight problem. Consequently the thought of objectively discovering absolute truth is perceived as unrealistic.

OUT

In view of this, postmoderns believe that we should endeavor to understand truth in context. What might be true in one context or culture might not be true in another. Because of the diverse worldviews that people possess, it is unrealistic to expect that some universal truth can apply to all people. Instead of *reason* being the chief way to deduce truth, *experience* becomes much more important. As far as postmoderns are concerned, truth is subjective and there is a plurality of ways to look at the world. Postmoderns do not have a problem with the supernatural, because they do not expect to be able to perceive and explain all things in a rational way. There is greater room for mysterious and unusual experiences.

Analyzing Postmodernity

Postmodernity gets a lot of bad press, especially from the moderns who do not like their neatly organized and packaged world being messed up. The reality is that both postmodernity and modernity have advantages and disadvantages. Because of the shift toward postmodernity, I believe it is especially important for us to understand postmodernity's strengths and weaknesses and see how these affect how we make disciples of Jesus Christ. As Christians in a postmodern context, we need to utilize the strengths and understand the weaknesses if we are going to do more than just survive.

Here is an example of the reality of postmodernity's strengths and weaknesses: Postmoderns are generally open to Jesus, will happily listen to what you have to say about Jesus, and are willing to receive the truth. However, they will just as happily receive a Buddhist's views on life, so it is difficult to know how much progress you are making in helping a postmodern person on his or her journey toward Christ. Realizing this difficulty can help you ask the right questions and give appropriate answers.

Christians have been put off by some negative impressions of postmodernity, and in some cases this is understandable, but we must not allow negative impressions to keep us from engaging with postmodernity in its true form. Some Christians, for example, react to the viewpoints of immature postmoderns who say things like, "There is no truth." But those people are not true ambassadors of postmodern thought; they are usually people who just like debating. If this is what Christians object to, they should look more deeply into what postmodernity is. Some other postmoderns are excessively into consumerism; pluralism allows them to be social chameleons who can believe one thing and act a certain way in one context but act like a completely different person in another context. They refuse to engage in any meaningful view of life and avoid any form of social responsibility. Such people would probably act this way even if they did not have postmodernity as an excuse. There is a simple, biblical word for this kind of lifestyle: selfishness.

In reality postmodernism has more to do with how people perceive and handle truth than with the selfishness associated with consumerism and pluralism. We cannot afford to ignore its impact, because its development as a philosophy has influenced culture in a way that has formed many of the younger generation. Postmodernity is more of a social state than a philosophy. It is the practical outworking of the postmodern philosophy in the lives of the everyday people around us. Whether or not you admit it, many of you reading this book right now have been shaped by postmodern culture.

I will not attempt to explain postmodernity as a social state in a few paragraphs of a single chapter. Instead, I think it would be more useful to highlight a few significant areas of interest regarding postmoderns, how they think and act, and how we can reach them.

Relationships

One of the great strengths I see in postmodernity is what some have called the tribal mind-set. The moderns heavily emphasized individuality and independence, but postmoderns love groups and have a strong desire to belong. This means that much of the influence on postmoderns occurs through relational networks.

A friend of mine runs a ministry with the young people in our city. I have been struck by the real sense of community that is displayed among these young people. I have observed some distinct "tribes" that have formed among them, and within these groups I have observed some strong friendships. The kids are affectionate with each other and care a lot about those who are part of the in-crowd. On the downside they can be quite cliquish, and getting to be a part of the group can be difficult and is sometimes discouraged by the in-crowd.

The strong sense of relationship and community for those within a group is interesting, considering that postmoderns focus on individual choice and personal belief. I believe there is a reason for this. Since postmoderns do not believe that truth is universal, it makes perfect sense to them for each person to be able to believe whatever he or she wants. It is from this openness to other people's beliefs that our pluralistic society has been birthed. A high value has been placed on tolerance. As far as postmoderns are concerned, every belief is equally valid as long it does not impeach someone else's belief and rights.

In a Christian context, the emphasis on relationships means that postmoderns will not easily jeopardize relationship because of theological differences. The value that is put on relationship forms a wonderful platform for unity. While in the past, moderns were likely to fall out over doctrine, this is less likely to happen in the case of postmoderns.

Community of shared experience

So what is it that holds such groups together?

For moderns, groups were held together and identity was formed by shared beliefs, but with postmoderns a greater emphasis is placed on shared experiences and interests. For example, among the young people mentioned above, there is the skater group, the BMX group, and the rock band group, among others. Each group has a focal point of interest that acts as the glue to hold the members together and make them distinct from other groups.

Because of the postmodern focus on relationship and the need to belong to a tribe, it is important for Christians to pursue discipleship within a community. This way postmoderns get to see truth in action. Even more than that, it means that we can earn the right to speak into their lives. Sometimes I hear people say, "You don't even know me. What gives you the right to preach at me?" As far as these people are concerned, unless you are in relationship with them, you have no right to speak into their lives. This is one of the reasons why postmoderns despise street preachers. I am not saying that street preaching from a soapbox never works, but I can tell you that the majority of young people I know have major issues with that form of evangelism.

The supernatural

Another point about postmoderns is that their openness to new experiences and beliefs has allowed them to be receptive to supernatural things. Postmoderns do not merely tolerate the supernatural; they actually pursue it. I believe this is fueled by a strong desire for self-discovery. Postmoderns recognize the uniqueness of each individual and seek fulfillment through realizing their dreams. Because they believe that people's identities are shaped by culture, many feel that they can be whatever or whoever they want to be. In one cultural context they are happy to be shaped one way, and in another context they are happy to be shaped another way. This chameleon-type approach to identity allows for an identity that is spiritual. Many postmoderns like the idea of an unseen world that influences the seen world, because they recognize that even as individuals they have a whole other world that is unseen and spiritual.

I think the popularity of the *Harry Potter* books and films is indicative of people's acquiescence to supernatural things. In addition to that, many young people today are into tarot cards, Ouija boards, and witchcraft, because they are aware of the reality of spiritual power. For them the supernatural is quite a normal thing. As we look around us, we see a proliferation of New Age and psychological opportunities for personal development and self-realization. This comes as no surprise at all because of the pursuit of the spiritual by many postmoderns.

A few years ago I was with some friends in a local shopping mall, and we were offering to pray for people. A young woman came up to us and asked for prayer. She said she had been messing around with a Ouija board and was now having trouble sleeping; she recognized some demonic activity in her life. Two things struck me about the encounter with this girl. First, she had obviously been curious enough about spiritual things to try out the board. And second, she had recognized that whatever power Christians had access to was able to deal with her problem.

This openness to the supernatural is a path for Christians to reach postmoderns. We shouldn't forget that although many moderns could handle what they saw as the good moral teachings

UP

DOWN

IN

OUT

of Jesus, they could not handle the idea of miracles. This resulted in many people rejecting the true gospel and instead accepting a watered-down version of Christianity that sought to explain the miracles of Jesus in plausible, rational ways. Postmodernity is an open door to present the gospel found in the Bible, with all its supernatural elements.

Language

Postmoderns have observed that language is used to construct reality, for both good and evil. In present times we use subtle changes in language to alter people's perception of reality. For example, think of the kind of language that is used to train soldiers for combat. It is much easier for a British soldier to "neutralize the target" than to take the lives of a bunch of young Iraqis. Another example would be the "termination of a fetus" as opposed to "killing a baby." I don't mean to be offensive or insensitive, but I think there would be far fewer abortions if potential mothers were told they were killing their unborn child rather than simply getting rid of some organic tissue—almost like removing an appendix or tonsils or some other seemingly dispensable organ.

The effects that subtle changes in language have on people's perception of reality have made postmoderns rather suspicious of language, and they are happy to deconstruct it. As they see it, language can be used to impose other people's beliefs upon them. They will always resent what they perceive as such imposition. Even a simple phrase like "the truth" is found to be offensive on multiple levels; not only does it imply that there is ultimate, absolute, universal truth, but it suggests superiority and a desire to bring others into conformity with one's view of reality. Such a position is deemed arrogant, if not oppressive.

It is therefore important for us to consider what language we use when we are preaching the gospel. If we use unfamiliar language, at the very least young people simply might not understand what the heck we are on about; but worse, they might reject what we say because they misunderstand us. I know that many people will reject Christ no matter what, but let it not be because of our poor communication.

At the risk of alienating some readers, I would like to give some examples of unhelpful Christian language. Asking postmoderns if they "are saved" means very little to them. Telling people they will "burn in hell" is neither friendly nor is it good news unless placed within the proper context. Excessive talk of "washing in blood" could get you arrested. And talk of being "slain in the spirit" might make people think they are about to be killed.

It is important that we learn to communicate what we really mean. It is not enough to throw around words that sound nice or that we heard at a church service. We are only truly communicating when people understand what it is we are trying to say. If you are actually trying to tell people that "God hates you and wants to torture you forever," then fair enough—I won't get in your way. I do assume, however, that most of us want to share *good* news.

Discipling Postmoderns

When I was at university studying psychology, I once had to write a review on articles related to minority influence. The core question I was asked to tackle was, how does a minority of people, including a single person, influence the majority? My study focused on three factors: the message, the messenger, and the

UP

DOWN

IN

OUT

method. I discovered that each of these factors needed to be just right for a minority to have any influence. One of my findings was that the messenger strongly had to live out the message in order for the message to get through to the recipient. Although this principle will always be true, I believe it is particularly relevant right now to sharing the gospel with postmoderns.

Postmoderns do not care for our theories on faith. To believe that our theories are true, they want to see them working in our lives. Moderns, however, took the message itself seriously; so if you could present a solid logical argument, you could influence people's beliefs. In this context, men like Ravi Zacharias and Josh McDowell were indispensable. Today these learned and masterful communicators would have little impact among many postmodern young people. Picture with me Josh McDowell giving a masterful talk on evidence for the resurrection of Jesus. He kindly offers to answer any questions from the floor. A scruffy teenager in the back of the theater stands up and asks, "So what?" Even if McDowell gave a perfect answer to the question, with some practical application, it would probably not hit home.

Postmoderns are much more influenced by seeing Christians living out truth on a daily basis. If we are going to preach love to them, they must see love. If we are going to preach transformation to them, they need to see transformation. If we are going to preach healing, then they will desperately desire to see healing.

I recall one of the early stages in my conversion. I had made an initial commitment to faith back in my home country of Sierra Leone and now found myself at a boarding school in the UK. At the time God was not uppermost in my mind, so I just got on with things and tried to fit in with my peers. Around Christmastime a cousin of mine invited me to join him for Christmas in Manchester. It was there that I met this wonderful family who I can honestly say transformed my life. This family did not just preach about God's love; they lived it. The mum took me in as a son and the daughters treated me like a brother. By now you are guessing that this might be my adopted Mum mentioned in an earlier chapter. You are correct. To cut a long story short, because of the actual display of God's love that I experienced from this family, I came into a life-transforming experience that resulted in my baptism and moving on to new levels of faith and ministry. Since my university days I have seen this principle of discipleship work not only in my own life but in the lives of many other young people.

You might have noticed that although on a number of occasions I have mentioned my coming to faith, I have not talked of a single "conversion experience." This is deliberate. Let me explain why.

Journey and Process

I have written this book with the intention that it be read primarily by young postmoderns. Let me explain how. One of my observations of postmoderns is that they connect with stories more than facts, with process more than single events. Because stories tend to convey a process with pivotal points along the way, they invite people on a journey rather than simply transfer information. Although postmoderns find the idea of a single *big* story rather restrictive, they are enthused by the idea of each person being on his or her own journey made up of his or her unique stories.

Many Christians who came to faith twenty or thirty years ago can give you the date and maybe even the time when they accepted Christ and became a Christian. I have found, however,

UP

DOWN

IN

OUT

that many young people today think more in terms of a journey of becoming a Christian rather than a specific moment when they became a Christian. I have even come across a postmodern poking fun at what he perceived as the ridiculous idea of someone saying they became a Christian on a specific date at a certain time.

Postmoderns seem more interested in the language of journey than that of crisis points. They do not seem to relate to people singling out a specific date and time as a point of conversion or "getting saved." There can be points on the journey where great progress is made, but it is a journey nonetheless. A simple line that one of my mentors taught me to ask people is, "Where are you on your spiritual journey?" He found that people always responded with surprise that he seemed to know that they *were* on a spiritual journey. One of the positive aspects of this approach is that it does not invalidate people's previous experiences and knowledge. Christians have a tendency to act as if everything anyone knows or has experienced before he or she hears about Jesus is unimportant. The truth is that our contribution to a person's spiritual journey is just another chapter in an unfolding story.

If we approach our evangelism with this in mind, not only will it remove the pressure on us to achieve more than we ever could in one meeting with a person; it will also reduce the risk of what some have termed "counterfeit" or "false" conversions. Billy Graham used to say that he never did mass evangelism, but rather personal evangelism on a mass scale. His point was that people come to know God not because of one event but because of the preparation that many friends and family have done in previous chapters of a person's story.

In this chapter I have focused on the issue of evangelizing post-moderns, and I acknowledge that this is specific to the culture I find myself working in today. My intention has not been to give a blow-by-blow account of how to evangelize and disciple post-moderns. Instead, I want to draw your attention to differences in people's worldviews that are worth exploring to effectively reach the world around us. Regardless of what nation or culture you find yourself in, it is important to consider some of its unique attributes and discover how they might affect *your* evangelism.

UP

DOWN

IN

OUT

Conclusion
The Manifesto

"The church needs another reformation." I remember the first time I heard someone say this. It was a weekday morning and a friend had turned up to my room rather excited about a dream from the previous night. As was usual, he told me about the dream, and then we both had to discern prayerfully whether his dream was a prophetic dream from God, a disturbance of sleep by the enemy, or an indication that my friend ate too much, too late the previous night. As my friend recounted the dream to me, my attention focused most closely on the end when he said, "The church needs another reformation." These words, he told me, had come from the most beautiful woman he had ever seen, dressed in a white wedding dress.

Our interpretation was that this woman was the bride of Christ speaking out prophetically about the church's need to return to simple, biblical truth and obey it. Although neither of us could be fully sure of the source of the dream, many Christians do believe that the church needs to become radical again. That is to say, the church needs to return to the roots of Christianity, namely, simple obedience. We need to get back to the basics and the fundamentals. The radical church is an obedient church.

If we define "reformation" as a fresh realization by the church of its need to obey God's words as revealed in Scripture, the church *does* need another reformation.

Luther's Reformation was in many ways also a revolution. Why do I say this? Well, I was struck by this thought when I watched the film *Luther*, starring Joseph Fiennes. Until that point, the significance of some of the violence that accompanied the Reformation had not fully dawned on me. I had read about it and heard about it, but seeing it in a visual form simply made me realize this was a revolution. The Reformation did not just have theological implications; it also had political ramifications. The more I thought about what I saw, the more I realized that Luther was not just a reformer but a revolutionary too. When we think about revolutions, we often think about some revolutionaries leading the way. These people tend to be driven by a set of values. And in order to be so passionate and focused, they need something—a manifesto. Luther's was his Ninety-five Theses.

Revolutions take place when massive change is needed. We need a revolution in the church today. Let me explain why I think this.

In the story of the wedding in Cana (John 2:1–13) we see a beautiful picture of how our lives should be. Mary, knowing who her son was and the authority and power he possessed, said to the servants, "Whatever he says to you, do it." The servants heeded her voice and followed the requests of Jesus without question or hesitation. Jesus said to the servants, "Fill the water pots with water," and they did. The passage says that "they filled them up to the brim." They did not fill them halfway. They filled them to the brim. Partial obedience would not have been good enough; at best it would have resulted in a partial miracle (they would only have had half-full pots of the wonderful wine that ensued).

I believe that many churches today are receiving only a partial blessing from God because of partial obedience. We are seeing a partial fulfillment of the promises of God. We see some wonderful promises in the New Testament. For example, Jesus promised that we who believe would do the same works and greater works than he did (John 14:12). Sadly, so many of us are not yet experiencing this. We are not doing what Jesus did, let alone *greater* works. Jesus also promised us that as believers we would cast out demons and speak in new languages (Mark 16:17–18), yet many churches are not experiencing any of this.

Seeing these promises fulfilled has to do with faith, because many times the promises are accompanied by phrases such as "if you believe." However, there is also the call to obey. Jesus points out that by faith we can see our prayer answered (Matt. 21:21–22), but also that for us to see our prayers answered, we must remain in him and his words must remain in us (John 15:7). Even Christ's promise to us that we can remain in his love is conditional on obeying his commandments (John 15:10).

For the body of Christ to be the effective community it was meant to be, and for the bride of Christ to become pure and spotless, we must return to teaching and obeying the *whole* counsel of God as revealed in the Scriptures.

In this book I have reminded us of some simple but important truths that we need to reconnect with if we are going to become effective disciples of Jesus. My hope is that like the servants at the wedding, we will become willing to trust and obey Jesus. Such trust and obedience have the power to transform the church.

The revolution that we need is a revolution of loving and obeying Jesus without reserve. If I could sum up my manifesto in a sentence, it would be something like this: I want to love Jesus so much that I obey his every word.

Epilogue

The scariest thing about writing this book is that it has taken many years to complete. During this time I have grown as a Christian, and some of my beliefs and values have developed— maybe even matured. It has taken a great deal of self-control (and a touch of laziness) to resist the temptation to rewrite some parts of the book. I feel that it captures a snapshot of where I was at the time of much of its conception. I am happy with where I was then, I am happy with where I am now, and I will be happy with wherever I will be in the future. It's all part of the unfurling journey of life with Christ.

With this in mind I would encourage people not to get too hot under the collar about anything they find offensive in this book. I would like to offend you just enough to maybe change your mind on a few issues but not enough for you to ignore everything else I have said. The good news is that this book contains general principles and ideas that remain core beliefs of mine. Although I might apply the principles a little differently now, they remain at the heart of my manifesto.

Further Reading

Section A

Bickle, Mike. *Passion for Jesus.* Lake Mary, Fla.: Charisma House, 2007.

This book helped me realize God's love for me and his desire for an intimate relationship with me.

Manning, Brennan. *The Ragamuffin Gospel.* Sisters, Ore.: Multnomah, 2000.

This book helped me understand grace expressed through God's unconditional love and forgiveness.

Swindoll, Charles. *The Grace Awakening.* Nashville: W Publishing, 2003.

This book not only communicates God's grace but challenges the reader to show grace to others as they have received it.

Yancey, Philip. *What's So Amazing about Grace.* Grand Rapids: Zondervan, 2003.

Another powerful book on grace. This book uses incredible storytelling to communicate profound truths about God's grace.

Section B

Burnell, Robert. *Escape from Christendom*. Minneapolis: Bethany Fellowship, 1980.

This book helped me examine my life to see what was genuine Christianity and love for God and what was possibly empty religion.

Cunningham, Loren. *Making Jesus Lord*. Seattle: YWAM Publishing, 1989.

Loren Cunningham challenges us to live a lifestyle of love, obedience, and sacrifice for the sake of Christ.

Drane, John. *The McDonaldization of the Church*. Macon, Ga.: Smyth & Helwys, 2001.

A book that highlights ways that the church has lost some of its ability to be unique and has instead opted for a one-size-fits-all approach to Christian life and worship.

Willard, Dallas. *The Divine Conspiracy*. San Francisco: HarperSanFrancisco, 1998.

A masterful work that examines many themes on Christian discipleship, with a particularly good exposition of the Sermon on the Mount.

Section C

Garrison, David. *Church Planting Movements*. Richmond, Va.: International Missions Board of the Southern Baptist Convention, 1999.

This inspiring book documents some recent church planting movements and some of the common factors that we can apply in our contact that may enable us to see similar growth.

Hogan, Brian. *There's a Sheep in My Bathtub: Birth of a Mongolian Church Planting Movement*. Bayside, Calif.: Asteroidea Books, 2007.

This adventurous and humorous book has some great church planting principles. Brian Hogan had a huge influence on me as I developed my thinking about church planting.

Miller, Rex. *The Millennium Matrix*. San Francisco: Jossey-Bass, 2004.

Rex Miller offers a more detailed analysis of church trends than I have. I found the way that Miller charts shifts in worldview very useful for understanding how the church has changed in the last few thousand years.

Patterson, George, and Richard Scoggins. *Church Multiplication Guide*. Revised edition. Pasadena: William Carey Library, 2003.

In my opinion, this is one of the best guides to church planting principles out there.

Viola, Frank. *Rethinking the Wineskin*. Third edition. Brandon, Fla.: Present Testimony Ministry, 2001.

As the name implies, this book challenges us to find fresh ways to look at the wineskin we call church. Frank Viola is a respected leader in the house church movement.

Section D

Cope, Landa. *Old Testament Template*. Burtigny, Switzerland: Template Institute, 2007.

Through Landa Cope's video series (later to become a book), I first encountered the challenge to preach the good news of the kingdom and to recognize God's hand in the spheres of our society.

Johnson, Bill. *The Supernatural Power of a Transformed Mind: Access to a Life of Miracles.* Shippensburg, Pa.: Destiny Image Publishers, 2005.

With plenty of testimonies to build your faith, this is a very practical and inspiring book for those who want to grow in their faith for a lifestyle of the supernatural.

Krallman, Gunter. *Leading with Jesus.* Buckinghamshire, UK: Authentic Lifestyle, 1998.

This was one of the first books I read on Christian leadership. It is challenging, focused, and concise. There is very little that Gunter does not cover in this small book.

McLaren, Brian. *A New Kind of Christian: A Tale of Two Friends on a Spiritual Journey.* San Francisco: Jossey-Bass, 2001.

Talk about messing with your head. This book forced me to explore the possibility that there are other ways to live out my Christian faith. McLaren is a genius at asking probing questions without asking probing questions.

Sheets, Dutch. *Intercessory Prayer.* Ventura, Calif.: Regal, 1996.

A well-loved book that contains practical tips for both budding and more mature Christians who desire to improve their intercessory prayer life.

About the Author

Born in Sierra Leone, Olu Robbin-Coker moved to the UK at age fifteen. After earning a BS in psychology from the University of St. Andrews, he completed a year of Bible training and a year of ministry under his pastor's mentoring, planting a youth and student congregation through his church.

In 2001 he attended a Discipleship Training School and joined Youth With A Mission (YWAM). Working out of the national office in West Kilbride, he developed a student ministry and then moved to Dundee to set up a mobile student ministry team. Feeling called to work among marginalized people, he and his wife, Ester, moved to the inner city and started an urban ministry team.

Olu presently leads the small urban ministry team in Dundee. He is part of the national leadership team of YWAM in Scotland and has an active speaking ministry that has taken him to Africa, Europe, North America, the Caribbean, and around the UK.

He and Ester have a desire to bless orphans and since 2004 have been fundraising for Living Way Children's Centre, which ministers to orphans and needy children in Sierra Leone.

Olu and Ester have three lovely kids: Rebekah, Sophia, and Daniel.